RAMEN NOODLE COOKBOOK

Delicious Recipes That Will Blow Your Mind

(The Highest Rated Yummy Ramen Noodle Cookbook)

Edward Halford

Published by Alex Howard

© **Edward Halford**

All Rights Reserved

Ramen Noodle Cookbook: Delicious Recipes That Will Blow Your Mind (The Highest Rated Yummy Ramen Noodle Cookbook)

ISBN 978-1-990169-77-9

All rights reserved. No part of this guide may be reproduced in any form without permission in writing from the publisher except in the case of brief quotations embodied in critical articles or reviews.

Legal & Disclaimer

The information contained in this book is not designed to replace or take the place of any form of medicine or professional medical advice. The information in this book has been provided for educational and entertainment purposes only.

The information contained in this book has been compiled from sources deemed reliable, and it is accurate to the best of the Author's knowledge; however, the Author cannot guarantee its accuracy and validity and cannot be held liable for any errors or omissions. Changes are periodically made to this book. You must consult your doctor or get professional medical advice before using any of the suggested remedies, techniques, or information in this book.

Table of contents

Part 1 1

Chapter 1: Savory Meals 2

1) Cheesy Rice 2

Thai Infused Ramen Bowl 4

Ramen Cacio E Pepe 5

Ramen With Kimchi 6

Chicken Sriracha Yakisoba 8

Ramen Taco Filling 10

Ramen And Cheese 11

Easy Ramen Beef And Broccoli 12

Garlicky Onion Ramen 13

Breakfast Ramen Mix Up 15

Veggies And Ramen Asian Stir Fry 16

No Rice Ramen Burritos 18

Burgers With Ramen Buns 20

Ramen Noodle And Pepper Jack Cheese 22

Ramen A La Carbonara 23

Taco Ramen Bowls 25

Pepperoni Pizza Ramen Skillet 26

Little Fuss Ramen Noodle Bowls 27

Chili & Ramen 28

Dressed Up Ramen For One 29

Coconut Shrimp Curry 30

Ramen Pizza Skillet 31

Cheesy Ramen Frittata 32

Chicken And Veggie Bowls 33

Shrimp Ro Mein 34

Mongolian Beef & Ramen 35

Kung Pao Ramen 37

Ramen Miso 39

Super Simple Surf And Turf Ramen Soup 41

Tofu & Mushroom Ramen Noodle Soup 42

Poor Man Rich Man Ramen 44

Ham & Cheese Noodles For One 46

Chicken With Peanuts Ramen Noodles 47

Coconut Shrimp Ramen 48

Compay Lemony-Herbed Chicken Ramen 51

Sloppy Ramens 52

Beef Tomato Noodle Skillet 53

Breakfast Burritos With A Kick 54

Fajitas A Ramen 55

Chicken Stroganoff On Ramen 56

Bacon % Chicken Ramen 57

Elegant Balsamic Ramen Chicken 58

Part 2	60
Ramen Burger	61
Ramen Noodle Burger: Bok Choy	64
Homemade Ramen Burger 3 (Bacon Flavored)	66
Ramen Turkey Burger 5	69
Vegan Eggplant Burger	71
Ramen Hisago Burger	76
Hisago Burger	78
Broccoli And Ramen Noodle Salad	81
Asian Noodles"N Shrimp	83
Coconut Curry Shrimp	85
Ramen'n Beef or Chicken with Veggies	87
Easy Noodle Salad	88
Ramen Noodle Casserole	90
Ramen Spam/ Ham	93
Chicken Broccoli Noodles	95
Top Ramen Noodle Cole Slaw	97
EASY ORIENTAL NOODLE SALAD	100
Sesame-Noodle Shrimp Salad	101
Japan Like A Pro	102
The Greatest Ever Juicy Juice Burger	105
Grilled T-Bone Steaks With Rub A Dub	107
The Whole Damn Chicken	109

2) Beef Stew 110

3) Lamb Stew 111

4) Chicken Gumbo 113

5) Baked Cauliflower With Cheese 115

6) Fried And Succulent Chicken Wings 117

7) Chunky And Homey Chicken And Noodle Soup 119

8) Chicken Pot Pie 121

9) Chicken Coated With Herbs And Served With Orzo 123

10) Chicken And Dumplings 125

11) Creamy Chicken Sauce For Pasta 126

12) Chicken Cacciatore 128

13) Baked Beans 130

14) Chicken Fricassee 132

15) Lentils In Honey 134

16) Crispy Fried Buttermilk Chicken 136

17) Cranberry And Bison Stew 138

18) Beef Stroganoff 140

19) Pot Roast 142

20) Vegetable Soup 144

Chapter 2: Desserts 146

21) Strawberry Shortcake 147

22) Shortcut To Apple Cobbler 149

23) Peanut Butter Bars 150

24) Peanut Butter And Apple Crisp	152
25) Marshmallow Cookie Bars	154
Easy Ramen Noodle Snacks	155
Fast Chicken Noodle Soup	155
Peanut Chicken Noodles	156
Rice And Shrimp	157
Spinach And Ramen Noodles	158
Vegan Ramen Salad	159
Veggie Ramen Ii	160
Foo Ramen	161
Chicken Salad	162
Mandarin Ramen Salad	163
Thai Ramen	164
Ramen Lasagna	165
Shrimp And Chili	166
Ham Fried Ramen Noodles	167
Parmesan Noodles	168
Homemade Chicken And Noodles	169
Semarang Kopyok Noodles	170
Riau Lendir Noodles	172
Makasar Titi Noodles	174
Malang Cwie Noodles	177
Kwetiau Fried Noodles	179

Javanese Kwetiau Fried Noodles 181

Fried Seafood Kwetiau Noodles 183

Chicken Fried Kwetiau Noodles 185

Shrimp Fried Rice Noodles 187

Part 1

Chapter 1: Savory Meals

1) Cheesy Rice

Ever tried cheese with rice?

Cooking Time: **10 minutes**

Makes: 8 servings

List of Ingredients:
- 1 ¼ cups of long grain rice
- 2 ½ cups of water
- 1 package (10 oz.) frozen spinach, thawed and drained
- 1 cup of cheddar cheese, grated
- 1 cup of half and half
- 1 tablespoon butter
- 1 teaspoon of salt
- ½ cup chopped onion

Procedure:

1. Add water to the pot and cook rice in it until tender and until most of the water has been absorbed.
2. Add all of the rest of the ingredients and give it a stir to mix.

3. Bake for 25 minutes in a low oven.

Thai Infused Ramen Bowl

1 package Ramen noodles
1 pack noodle flavoring
1 tablespoon soy sauce
2 tablespoons chunky peanut butter
2 teaspoons Sriracha chili sauce
1/2 scallion, thinly sliced (optional)

Boil noodles with flavor pack and drain off most liquid. Toss with soy sauce, peanut butter, and Sriracha. Garnish with scallion. Eat immediately.

Ramen Cacio E Pepe

2 packages instant ramen

1 package frozen peas

3 tablespoons butter

1 tablespoon olive oil

1 cup Pecorino Romano

1 cup Parmigiano Reggiano

Fresh ground pepper

In a pot add the water, butter, olive oil and a good amount of black pepper, also add frozen peas.

Bring to a boil, stir and reduce to a simmer when boiling.

Add cheese and stir, then quickly add the ramen.

Mix up the noodles and when they separate, constantly stir them until the noodles are soft and well dressed.

Serve in a bowl and add more fresh ground pepper on top.

Ramen With Kimchi

Serves:2
3 cups water
½ cup well fermented kimchi
¼ cup bean sprouts
1 tablespoon white rice wine
1 teaspoon extra light olive oil
1 teaspoon sesame oil
1 teaspoon rice vinegar
1 teaspoon smoked paprika
1 teaspoon low sodium soy sauce
½ teaspoon Korean red chili flakes
¼ teaspoon Himalayan/sea salt
A few sprinkles Szechuan peppercorns
2 packets organic ramen
Garnish
1 scallion
1-2 tablespoons well fermented kimchi

Add the 3 cups of water, kimchi, bean sprouts, white rice wine, olive oil, sesame oil, rice vinegar, paprika, soy sauce, Korean red chili flakes, salt, Szechuan peppercorns and ramen in a small/medium saucepan.

Bring it to a boil, and continue to cook on boiling heat for a total of 8-10 minutes until the ramen is soft to eat.

Meanwhile, slice the scallions into super thin strips and put it in ice water for a few seconds to let it curl up a bit.

Once the ramen is ready, spoon it onto one or two bowls, then garnish with the scallion and a tablespoon or two of fresh kimchi.

Chicken Sriracha Yakisoba

Serves: 6

½ head green cabbage
1 medium yellow onion
2 medium carrots
1 small crown broccoli
2 inches fresh ginger
1 large chicken breast
2 Tbsp vegetable oil
2 (3 oz.) packages ramen noodles
seasoning packets discarded
1 tsp sesame oil (optional)
¼ cup soy sauce
¼ cup worcestershire sauce
2 Tbsp ketchup
(up to) 1 Tbsp sriracha hot sauce
1 Tbsp sugar

Before you begin, prepare the meat and vegetables for stir frying. Peel the ginger with either a vegetable peeler or the side of a spoon and then grate it with a cheese grater. Peel and grate the carrots with a large holed cheese grater. Remove the core from the cabbage and cut into thin strips. Slice the onion into thin strips. Cut the broccoli into bite-sized pieces. Slice the chicken into thin strips.

Begin boiling a medium pot full of water for the noodles. Heat the vegetable oil in a large skillet over medium-high heat. When the oil is hot, add the grated ginger, saute for about 30 seconds to one minute (its okay if it sticks to the pan but don't let it burn). Add the chicken strips and cook until they are no longer pink (about five minutes).

Once the chicken is cooked through, add all of the vegetables. Stir and cook until wilted (about 5-10 minutes). Meanwhile, once the water boils, add the noodles and cook just until tender (2-3 minutes). Drain, return to the pot (with the heat turned off) and toss with the sesame oil to keep from sticking.

In a small bowl, combine the soy sauce, worcestershire sauce, ketchup, sriracha, and sugar. Use only ½ tsp of sriracha if you don't want it spicy, use up to 1 Tbsp if you like it hot. Stir until the ketchup and sugar are dissolved. Pour the sauce into the skillet with the chicken and vegetables with the heat still on medium high. Add the noodles, stir to coat everything in the sauce, and heat through (just a few minutes).

Ramen Taco Filling

1/2 lb ground beef
1 pkg ramen beef flavor
1 cup water
1 pkg taco seasoning
Taco shells and desired toppings;
Cheese
tomatoes
olives
lettuce
onions
sour cream
salsa

Cook up ground beef, then add a pack of raw crunched-up ramen noodles along with the water and seasoning packet to the skillet. Cook it down until the ramen is the desired texture, adding more water as necessary. Scoop it into taco shells, top as desired, and chow down.

Ramen And Cheese

1 pkg cooked chicken flavor ramen
1/2 block of Processed Block Cheese Spread
1/2 c milk
2 T butter

Use a half block of Velveeta mixed with some milk and butter (heat it up in the microwave until melted and combined). Combine the cooked noodles with the cheese sauce, top with more cheese, and broil until brown and bubbly.

Easy Ramen Beef And Broccoli

3/4 lb. skirt or flank steak
1/3 c. low-sodium soy sauce
2 cloves garlic, minced
Juice of 1 lime
1 tsp. honey
1/2 tsp. cayenne pepper
1 onion, diced
2 bell peppers, sliced
1 head broccoli, florets removed
3 packs boiled ramen noodles (seasoning packets discarded)

In a large skillet over medium-high heat, heat oil. Add steak and sear until your desired doneness, about 6 minutes per side for medium, then transfer to a cutting board and let rest, 5 minutes. Slice.

In a small bowl, whisk together soy sauce, garlic, lime juice, honey, and cayenne until combined and set aside. Add onion, peppers, and broccoli to skillet and cook until tender, 6 minutes, then add soy sauce mixture and stir until fully coated. Add cooked ramen noodles and steak and toss until combined. Serve.

Garlicky Onion Ramen

Serves: 4

3 Pkg Ramen Noodles any flavor
4 cloves garlic
½ bunch green onions
4 Tbsp butter
2 tsp soy sauce
2 Tbsp brown sugar
1 tsp sesame oil
2 Tbsp oyster sauce

Add the oyster sauce, brown sugar, soy sauce and sesame oil to a bowl and stir until combined.

Bring a large pot of water to a boil and cook the noodles according to the package directions. Drain the cooked noodles in a colander, then set aside.

Mince the garlic and slice the green onions. Melt the butter in a large skillet over medium-low heat. Once the butter is melted and bubbly, add the garlic and onions (save a few for garnish) and sauté until they are soft and fragrant.

Remove the skillet from the heat. Add the drained ramen and oyster sauce mixture to the skillet, and stir well to coat the ramen. If your ramen is stiff or sticky making it hard to stir, sprinkle a small amount of hot water over the ramen to loosen it up. Garnish the ramen with any reserved sliced green onions, then serve.

Breakfast Ramen Mix Up

2 ramen packs (seasoning packets discarded)
4 slices bacon, chopped into 1/2-in pieces
2 eggs
1 c. shredded sharp Cheddar
2 scallions, sliced
Sriracha or other hot sauce (optional)
1 tsp. olive oil
ground pepper

Boil noodles according to package instructions. Save 1/4 c. of cooking water to loosen sauce later, if needed. Drain noodles, toss with oil so they don't stick.

Heat medium skillet over medium heat. Cook bacon pieces until brown and crisp.

Add the noodles to the skillet and coat with bacon and bacon fat. Turn off the heat.

Beat eggs with fork. Mix in cheese.

Pour egg-cheese mixture to skillet and toss with bacon and noodles.

Divide between bowls. Garnish with scallions, fresh ground pepper and a drizzle of hot sauce, if desired.

Veggies And Ramen Asian Stir Fry

for the sauce:
2 tablespoon rice vinegar
2 tablespoon sesame oil
4 tablespoons soy sauce
1 tablespoon hoisin sauce
2 teaspoon brown sugar
2 teaspoon garlic powder
2 teaspoon ground ginger
for the ramen noodle stir fry:
5 packs of ramen noodles (discard the flavor packets)
2 tablespoon olive oil
1 clove garlic, minced
1 teaspoon ground ginger
3.5 ounces shiitake mushrooms, sliced
1 small head of broccoli, cut into florets
1 cup shredded carrots
1 tablespoon minced cilantro

Whisk all of the sauce ingredients together in a bowl until well combined. Set aside.

Bring a large pot of water to boil over high heat, and cook the ramen according to the directions on the package.

Heat the olive oil in a large skillet over medium-high heat. Add the minced garlic, ground ginger, mushrooms, broccoli, and carrots, and saute for 4-6 minutes.

Drain the ramen and add the noodles to the skillet. Add the sauce & cilantro to the skillet. Mix well and cook for 1-2 minutes to warm sauce.

No Rice Ramen Burritos

For the ramen:
1 package ramen noodles
2 tablespoons peanut oil
1/2 teaspoon minced garlic
2 tablespoons chopped cilantro

For the ramen burrito:
3 burrito-size flour tortillas, warmed

Optional toppings:
Guacamole
Shredded cheddar cheese
Shredded chicken
Spam, diced
Pico de gallo
Corn, cut off the cob
Fried egg
Sriracha
Ranch dressing
Refried beans

Make the ramen: Boil 2 cups of water in a medium saucepan; once the water comes to a boil, break the ramen into 4 chunks and add the ramen noodles and half of the seasoning packet to the water; cook for two minutes. Drain.

Add oil, garlic, and cilantro to a skillet set over high heat, and heat for about a minute, or until the garlic is sizzling. Add noodles and the other half of the seasoning packet. Cook for an additional minute until the noodles are warmed through.

Assemble: Add 1/4 cup of noodles to a warmed tortilla, and fill it with your choice of toppings. Roll up the burrito. Repeat with remaining ingredients, and serve immediately.

Burgers With Ramen Buns

2 packets of instant ramen noodles
½ lb ground beef
1 garlic glove, crushed
½ to 1 tablespoon fish sauce
½ teaspoon black pepper
¼ teaspoons sugar
sesame oil
arugula or lettuce
scallion

SHOYU SAUCE(or just use a splash of soy sauce, your call).
¼ cup soy sauce
¼ cup brown sugar
1 garlic, crushed,
½ cm piece of ginger, grated
1 shallot or ¼ small onion, chopped
½ teaspoon cornstarch dissolved in 1 teaspoon water

For the ramen bun,
 Cook your ramen (without the seasoning packet). Drain through a colander and don't rinse with cold water. While still hot, divide the ramen into four

portions, and place each portion in [very. we're talking 1-2 drops of oil] lightly greased ramekins or other round containers to mold the ramen into a round shape. Place a smaller, heavier bowl over the ramen to press it into shape. Refrigerate for at least 15 minutes.

If you're using the beef patty recipe, combine ground beef, garlic, fish sauce, sugar and black pepper.Gently form meat into a balls, then flatten into patties. Refrigerate until needed.

For the shoyu sauce,

Combine all the ingredients except the dissolved cornstarch, and bring to a boil, When it has slightly reduced, stir in the cornstarch and turn off the heat. Set aside.

Heat a tablespoon of sesame oil in a pan, and fry both ramen patties until brown on one side and cooked on the other. Set aside, ready for the hamburger, with a bit of arugula or lettuce on one side.

Fry your hamburger patty as you like it. Glaze it with the shoyu sauce and sesame oil to taste.

Place cooked hamburger patty on top of the bun with the arugula or lettuce, spoon some more shoyu sauce and top with scallions.

Ramen Noodle And Pepper Jack Cheese

4 (3 oz.) packages of Ramen Noodles (noodles only)
1 Tbsp. butter
1 Tbsp. flour
1½ cups milk
1 (8 oz.) package (2 cups) Pepper Jack Cheese, shredded
2 tsps. Siracha sauce
½ tsp. salt

Bring a pot of water to boil and add noodles. Boil 1 minute, or 1 minute 15 seconds.

Drain in a colander and rinse with cold water. Spray a little oil and toss them around with your hands breaking them up.

Heat butter in a large saucepan on medium heat and add flour to make a roux. Cook about a minute.

Pour in the milk and cook until it becomes frothy and thick, stir occasionally.

Reduce heat to low and gradually add cheese.

Add Sriracha and salt and stir until cheese is melted.

Increase heat to medium to medium/low and add noodles. Cook until heated through, about 1-2 minutes. Add milk a Tbsp. at a time if you want the sauce to be thinner.

Ramen A La Carbonara

1 egg

1 egg yolk

1/3 cup parmesan cheese

Some ground pepper

2 strips of bacon, sliced in

1 packet instant ramen

1-2 tablespoons of extra virgin olive oil

In a small bowl, add one whole egg, one egg yolk, 1/3 cup parmesan cheese, and pepper to taste. Whisk with fork until well combined.

Cut two strips of bacon crosswise into half-inch strips. Fry until cooked but not yet crispy.

Boil water and cook ramen very al dente, or just until it can be loosened from it's block form.

Add 1-2 tablespoons of olive oil to the bacon and stir, lifting any bacon bits that are stuck to the pan. Once the oil is hot, remove the pan from heat. Pour a small amount of the water the ramen was cooked in and stir. Add the ramen noodles and stir some more, coating the noodles in the bacon/olive oil mixture. Next, add the egg mixture, making sure to pour it onto the noodles and not straight onto the pan. Stir vigorously.

The heat from the pan and ingredients need to turn the egg mixture into a creamy sauce but if the eggs get too hot they will cook too much and become scrabbled eggs. Add additional ramen water as needed to create a smooth but creamy sauce.

Plate and top with additional Parmesan cheese and pepper.

Taco Ramen Bowls

1 packet ramen noodles, beef flavor
1 (15 ounce) can diced tomatoes
1/2 cup water
2 tablespoons taco seasoning mix
1/2 cup canned chicken
1/2 cup sweet corn
1/2 cup cheddar cheese, shredded
1/4 cup cilantro

In a large pot, bring ramen noodles, half of the ramen beef seasoning packet, diced tomatoes, and water to a boil. Cook until the noodles are softened, about 3 minutes. Remove from heat and pour into two serving bowls.

Sprinkle remaining ramen beef seasoning over the canned chicken. Place half of the chicken on top of the ramen in each bow.

Heat corn in a small, microwave safe bowl until warm, about 1 minute. Place on top of ramen in each bowl.

Top each bowl with cheddar cheese and cilantro. Serve.

Pepperoni Pizza Ramen Skillet

2 packages (3 oz each) beef-flavor ramen noodle soup mix
1 lb lean ground beef
24 slices pepperoni
1 can (14.5 oz) diced tomatoes with basil, garlic and oregano, undrained
1 cup water
1 small green bell pepper, cut into 1/2-inch pieces
1 cup shredded mozzarella cheese

Break blocks of noodles in half (reserve one seasoning packet; discard second packet); set aside. In 10-inch skillet, cook beef and pepperoni over medium heat 8 to 10 minutes, stirring occasionally, until beef is brown; drain.

Stir tomatoes, water and reserved seasoning packet into beef mixture. Heat to boiling. Stir in noodles and bell pepper. Cook 3 to 5 minutes, stirring occasionally, until noodles are tender.

Sprinkle cheese on noodle mixture in ring around edge of skillet. Cover and let stand about 5 minutes or until cheese is melted.

Little Fuss Ramen Noodle Bowls

2 teaspoons vegetable oil
1 lb boneless beef sirloin steak, cut into thin strips
2 cups water
1 package (3 oz) Oriental-flavor ramen noodle soup mix
1 pkg (1 lb) fresh stir-fry vegetables (broccoli, cauliflower, celery, carrots, snow pea pods and bell peppers) (4 cups)
1/4 cup stir-fry sauce or 1 Tablespoon in ¼ cup water soy sauce

In 12-inch skillet, heat oil over medium-high heat. Add beef; cook 3 to 5 minutes, stirring occasionally, until brown. Remove beef from skillet.

In same skillet, heat water to boiling. Break block of noodles from soup mix into water; stir until slightly softened. Stir in vegetables. Heat to boiling. Boil 5 to 7 minutes, stirring occasionally, until vegetables are crisp-tender.

Stir in contents of seasoning packet from soup mix, the stir-fry sauce and beef. Cook 2 to 3 minutes, stirring frequently, until hot. Serve in individual bowls.

Chili & Ramen

Servings: 1

1 can of your favorite chili
Ramen
water

Same process as the one above, except this time take out excess water and pour in the chili.
Add cheese if you're feeling elegant.

Dressed Up Ramen For One

Servings:**1**

2 cups water
½ medium onion, sliced
¼ cup mushrooms, sliced
¼ cup bok choy (or other greens), chopped
¼ cup frozen corn
1 package instant ramen noodles
1 egg
2 scallions, cut into 2-inch pieces

1. Bring water to a boil in medium pot.
2. Add noodles to boiling water and cook for about3 minutes.
3. Stir in flavor package. Discard dried vegetable package and stir in fresh and frozen vegetables.
4. Crack raw egg into soup and push it toward the bottom to cook in the hot broth.
5. Let everything simmer until onions, bok choy and corn are cooked through, and mushrooms and scallions are tender. The egg should be cooked enough that the exterior is white.

Coconut Shrimp Curry

2 packages ramen noodles soup mix (any flavor)
½ c. light coconut milk
⅓ c. creamy peanut butter
2 tbsp. fresh lime juice
¼ tsp. red pepper flakes (optional)
1 lb. cooked, cleaned, peeled and deveined large shrimp
½ 1/2 seedless cucumber
4 scallions
Lime wedges, for serving

Bring 4 cups water to a boil in a large skillet. Break each package of noodles into 4 sections; add to boiling water (save seasoning packets for another use). Cover skillet, remove from heat and let stand 5 minutes.

Meanwhile, in a large bowl, whisk together the coconut milk, peanut butter, lime juice and red pepper (if using).

Drain noodles. Add them to the bowl with the dressing along with the shrimp, cucumber and scallions and toss to combine. Serve with lime wedges, if desired

Ramen Pizza Skillet

Serves: 6

8 c. water

4 package any flavor ramen noodle soup

1 tbsp. olive oil

1 c. spaghetti sauce

4 oz. mozzarella cheese

17 slice pepperoni

½ tsp. dried oregano

Heat broiler. Bring water to boil in a 2 1/2- to 3 1/2-quart pot. Add noodles and cook, stirring occasionally, 3 minutes or until tender. Drain in a colander.

Heat olive oil in a large skillet. When hot, add noodles and press evenly to cover bottom of pan. Cook 2 minutes or until browned underneath.

Spread sauce over noodles, then sprinkle with cheese, pepperoni and oregano.

If skillet handle is plastic or wood, wrap it in a double layer of foil to protect it from scorching. Broil 4 to 5 inches from heat source 2 minutes or until top is bubbly and cheese starts to brown. Let cool about 5 minutes before cutting in wedges to serve.

Cheesy Ramen Frittata

Serves: 6

2 c. frozen green peas

3 package any flavor ramen noodle soup

1 container part-skim ricotta cheese

3 large eggs

½ c. milk

½ c. Grated Parmesan cheese

¼ tsp. Pepper

1 can chunky tomatoes

Heat oven to 400°F. Lightly grease a 13 x 9-inch baking dish.

Bring a half-filled 4- to 6-quart pot of water to boil. Add frozen peas and return to a boil. Break up noodles as directed on package and add to pot. Cook 3 minutes, stirring occasionally, or until noodles and peas are tender. Drain in a colander.

Meanwhile stir ricotta, eggs, milk, Parmesan, pepper and the 2 seasoning packets in a large bowl until blended. Stir in noodles and peas.

Transfer mixture to prepared baking dish and spread evenly. Bake about 20 minutes or until set.

Heat tomatoes in a saucepan or microwave until hot. Spoon over frittata. Cut in squares to serve.

Chicken And Veggie Bowls

Serves: 4

3 tablespoons olive oil
8-oz. package mushrooms, chopped
2 cups broccoli florets
2 cloves garlic, minced
1/4 cup fresh flat-leaf parsley, chopped
Salt and pepper, to taste
48 oz. chicken stock
2 cups shredded, cooked chicken (suggestion: pull meat from a Rotisserie chicken)
2 packages Ramen noodles

Heat olive oil in a large skillet or Dutch oven over medium heat. Add mushrooms, broccoli, garlic, parsley, salt and pepper. Cook for 5 minutes, or until veggies are fragrant and begin to get soft.

Add chicken stock and bring to a boil over high heat. Simmer over medium-low heat for 5 minutes. Add chicken and Ramen noodles and simmer for an additional 5-7 minutes, or until noodles are cooked through. Serve warm!

Shrimp Ro Mein

Serves: 6 servings

1 large white onion, diced
2 stalks celery, diced
1 large zucchini, quartered and then diced
1 bell pepper, diced
3 packages oriental flavored ramen
2 pounds uncooked shrimp, shelled and de-veined

In a large pan on medium high heat, add 2 tablespoons sunflower seed oil until shimmery.

Add onion, pepper and celery until slightly soft.

Add zucchini and cook until all vegetables are browned.

Add 8 ounces of water, noodles and spice packets from ramen packages, cover.

After about 6 minutes, check to see if noodles have softened- not enough to be ready, but enough to move around the pan without breaking them. Stir around pan and add shrimp.

Cook for another 5-8 minutes, until shrimp are a nice, even pink- tossing as it cooks to ensure even heat.

Top with siracha, green onions, or anything you typically like with lo mein!

Mongolian Beef & Ramen

Serves: 4

1½ lb flank steak
¼ cup cornstarch
¼ cup vegetable oil
1 green bell pepper, sliced into thin strips
8 oz dry ramen noodles
3 green onions, chopped
For Sauce
2 tbsp sesame oil
¾ cup soy sauce, low sodium
⅔ cup brown sugar
1¼ cup chicken broth
4 cloves garlic, minced
¼ tsp red pepper flakes

Slice the flank steak into small thin pieces against the grain. In a large resealable bag add the starch and the beef to it. Close the ziploc bag and shake really well until each pieces is coated with cornstarch.

In a non stick skillet heat the oil. When the oil is hot, add beef and cook until browned. It will take 2 or 3 batches because you don't want the steak pieces to stick to each other. Also if you need more oil after the batch feel free to add more. Remove beef from skillet to a plate and empty the oil from the skillet.

Add the bell pepper to the skillet and saute it for a couple minutes just until it gets soft. Remove the pepper from the skillet to a plate and set aside.

In that same skillet add sauce ingredients, the sesame oil, soy sauce, brown sugar, garlic, chicken broth and red pepper flakes. Stir and cook over medium heat until sauce thickens a bit and reduces by about a quarter. It took me about 10 minutes until the sauce thickened and reduced. You don't want to reduce it too much because you need more sauce for the noodles.

In the meantime cook the ramen noodles according to package instructions.

Return the beef and bell pepper to the skillet and toss in the sauce. Add the cooked ramen noodles to the skillet and toss everything together. Top with green onions and serve.

Kung Pao Ramen

4 servings
1 Tbsp olive oil or vegetable oil
1 red bell pepper, chopped
6 green onions, divided
2 cloves garlic, minced
4 cups water
1 (14.5 oz) can low-sodium chicken broth
2 - 3 Tbsp sriracha
1 1/2 Tbsp rice vinegar
1 Tbsp oyster sauce
2 (3.77 oz) pkgs Oriental Flavor Ramen
2 1/2 cups shredded or diced cooked chicken breast or thighs
1/2 cup unsalted dry roasted peanuts
Sesame seeds (optional)

Heat oil in a large pot over medium-high heat. Add bell pepper and four of the chopped green onions and saute 2 minutes, then add garlic and saute 1 minute longer. Stir in water, chicken broth, sriracha, rice vinegar and oyster sauce and bring to a boil. Once it reaches a boil add Oriental flavored ramen noodles, cover and boil 4 minutes. Pour seasonings from package into a bowl and ladle out two cups of the soups broth into the bowl and stir, then return to pan. Stir in cooked chicken. Sprinkle each serving with peanuts, sesame seeds and remaining green onions. Serve warm

Ramen Miso

Serves: 2

2 cup napa cabbage, shredded or finely chopped
⅓ cup carrots, peeled and cut into thin strips (julienned)
2 tbsp vegetable oil
2 garlic cloves, finely chopped
1 tbsp ginger, peeled and finely chopped
3 scallions, finely chopped
2 packages/squares dry ramen noodles (egg noodles)
4 cups chicken stock
2 boiled eggs or soy pickled eggs

For the miso tare:
1 tsp Korean chili bean sauce
¼ cup red miso paste
2 tbsp sake
3 tbsp mirin
1 tsp sesame oil

- Bring a medium size pot of water to boil.
- Mix the ingredients for the miso tare in a bowl and set aside.

- Heat up chicken stock.

- In a medium size pan over high heat, add oil, garlic and ginger and cook for 1 minute.

- Add cabbage and carrots and cook for 2 minutes until carrots are tender but still yielding a crunch. Set aside.

- When water is boiling, add ramen noodles and cook and follow instructions according to package (usually about 3 minutes). Drain and set aside.

- In a soup bowl, divide miso tare evenly (2 tbsp each).

- Divide ramen noodles evenly and add chicken stock (2 cups each bowl).

- Stir well, top with scallions, cabbage and carrots, and pickled eggs. Serve miso ramen immediately.

Super Simple Surf And Turf Ramen Soup

Serves: 1

2 chicken flavored ramen

3.5 shiitake mushrooms

½ pound uncooked frozen shrimp

6 mini frozen meatballs

6 oz. spinach

2 tablespoons soy sauce

sriracha

Add 2 quarts of water to a pot and then bring to a boil.

Once the water is boiling add the flavor packets, noodles, shrimp, meatballs and mushrooms.

Stir until the noodles and shrimp are cooked and the meatballs are heated through.

Turn off the heat and then add the spinach and soy sauce. Stir to combine.

Serve. Add sriracha to taste.

Tofu & Mushroom Ramen Noodle Soup

2 eggs, poached
3.5 ounces shiitake mushrooms, sliced
1 Tablespoon unsalted butter
1 Tablespoon soy sauce26 ounces vegetable stock
1/2 teaspoon ground ginger
1/2 package firm tofu, cubed
1 carrot, peeled and sliced
1 celery stalk, sliced
1-2 kale greens, rib removed and chopped
mini bell peppers, sliced
green onions, sliced thin (optional)
ramen noodles, uncooked

Poach eggs in medium-sized saucepan. Rinse pan and fill with water and return to stove. Bring water to a boil (for ramen noodles).

Saute shiitake mushrooms in butter and soy sauce for 5 minutes in a non-stick pan. Set aside.

Add vegetable stock to large pot and add ground ginger. Turn heat to medium high and bring to a boil. Allow to boil for 5 minutes and lower heat and allow to simmer. Add tofu, carrot and celery stalk.

In original saucepan, add ramen noodles and cook according to package instructions. Drain and add noodles to bowl. Arrange bowls with kale, mini bell peppers and poached egg. Pour broth on top (and add tofu, celery and carrots) and garnish with green onions. Serve immediately.

Poor Man Rich Man Ramen

- 4 packs of Chicken flavored, Spicy ramen noodles
- 9 oz beef smoked sausage, chopped (or 4 beef hotdogs)
- 1 yellow onion, chopped
- 1 red anaheim pepper
- 1/2 green bell pepper, chopped
-1/2 red bell pepper, chopped
-1 tsp fresh chopped garlic
- Canola oil
-Mesquite Seasoning
-Chipotle Seasoning
Crushed red pepper

Heat skillet halfway between medium and medium-high

Generously coat large skillet with canola oil, add garlic.

 Add peppers and onions to skillet.

Add 1/2 tsp of mesquite seasoning and 1/2 tsp southwest chipotle seasoning to skillet

Open ramen packages and add flavor sachets to 2/3 pot of water DO NOT ADD NOODLES YET.

Bring water to boil on high heat.

While waiting for water to boil, stir skillet with peppers, onion, and seasoning. continue stirring on occasion.

Once water begins to boil in pot, add ramen noodles.

Add sausage (or hot dogs) to skillet.

Cook noodles until desired tenderness, then transfer to colander to drain.

Stir skillet, mixing seasoning, meat, and vegetables.

Once noodles have drained, transfer noodles from colander to skillet.

Increase heat on skillet to medium-high and fry noodles with meat, seasoning, and vegetables. STIR SKILLET CONTINUOUSLY.

Add oil to keep noodles from sticking together.

If desired, add an additional 1/2 tsp of mesquite seasoning and 1/2 tsp of southwest chipotle seasoning for more intense flavor.

Remove skillet from heat, stir and serve.

Ham & Cheese Noodles For One

Servings 1

1 (3 ounce) package pork-flavored ramen noodles

3 -4 ham slices, thin lunchmeat style

1/4 cup cheddar cheese, grated (or to taste)

1 cup water

Pour 1 cup water in a pan.

Put noodles in water.

Set noodles and water to boiling.

Once noodles have broken up rip the ham in little bite size pieces and place over the noodles.

Just before too much water evaporates remove from stove. Just about a tablespoon or 2 of water leftover.

Add seasoning packet and stir around well.

Top with cheese, let melt and enjoy

Chicken With Peanuts Ramen Noodles

2 Packages Chicken Ramen Noodles – noodle only

1 Cup Shredded Chicken

4 Green Onions Sliced Thin

1 Tablespoon Crunchy Peanut Butter

1 Tablespoon Teriyaki Sauce

Cook noodles on stovetop as directed minus the flavor packets. In large skillet, mix together peanut butter and teriyaki sauce until smooth. Add in shredded chicken and onions cooking for 3-4 minutes. Toss with ramen noodles and serve.

Coconut Shrimp Ramen

2 Packages Shrimp Ramen Noodles – noodle only
½ Cup Coconut Milk
2 Teaspoons Crunchy Peanut Butter
Juice of 1 Lime
4 Green Onions Sliced
1 Clove Garlic Crushed
1/4 Teaspoon Red Pepper Flakes
1 Pound Shrimp {cleaned & deveined}

Cook noodles on stovetop as directed minus the flavor packets. Drain and set noodles aside. In large skillet cook shrimp 3-4 minutes on each side until cooked through, remove from skillet and toss with noodles. Pour milk, peanut butter, lime, garlic and red pepper flakes into skillet stirring until well blended. Add in green onions and cook on medium heat for 2-3 minutes. Pour over noodles and shrimp and toss until well coated.

Ramen Veggie Ribbon Salad

Prepare ramen according to package directions; drain. Chill noodles. Make zucchini and carrot ribbons with a vegetable peeler. Toss noodles and vegetable ribbons with vinaigrette.

Quick n Easy Curry

Prepare ramen according to package directions, except replace water with 1 cup coconut milk (from the Dairy section); stir in curry powder and seasoning packet.

Sparamen and Meatballs

Prepare ramen according to package directions; drain. Stir in pasta sauce and cooked Italian Meatballs (from the Frozen section). Heat until warm.

Chili Cheese Dog Ramen

Prepare ramen according to package directions; drain. Top noodles with cooked hot dog, chili and cheddar cheese. Heat until warm.

Super Quick Pad Thai Ramen

Prepare ramen according to stovetop directions, except use 1 cup water. Break ramen into small pieces, and add desired amount of cooked shrimp (we used Market Pantry Fully Cooked Salad Shrimp from the Freezer section). Cover and cook 3 minutes until noodles have softened. Stir in chopped peanuts, fresh lime juice, soy sauce, honey and seasoning packet; simmer an additional minute until sauce has thickened. Top with fresh cilantro.

Ramen Frittata for Two

Divide finely crushed uncooked noodles between two microwave-safe mugs. Stir 1 lightly beaten egg, 1/2 cup milk, shredded cheddar cheese and seasoning packet in small bowl. Pour evenly into mugs. Microwave 1 1/2 to 2 minutes on HIGH until cooked through; let stand 1 minute. Top each with a slice of bacon.

Compay Lemony-Herbed Chicken Ramen

1 package Roast Chicken or Chicken flavored ramen
1/3 cup leftover roast chicken
2 tablespoons lemon juice
1/4 cup shredded carrots
2 sprigs fresh thyme.

Boil the ramen according to package directions and add the seasoning packet.

While the ramen is cooking, shred the chicken with two forks or by hand.

When the ramen is finished, pour it into a bowl. Stir in the chicken, shredded carrots and lemon juice. Pull the thyme leaves off the sprigs and into the bowl.

Parmesan Ramen

1 package any flavor ramen noodles
2 cups water
1/4 cup Parmesan cheese

What to do:
Cook noodles according to package directions and drain. sprinkle
with Parmesan.

Sloppy Ramens

3 packs Ramen noodles any flavor
3 or 4 Tbsp. Sloppy Joe Seasoning Mix
1 lb. Ground Beef
2 quarts Canned Diced Tomatoes with juice
1/2 or 1 cup Water
1 cup Frozen Chopped Bell Peppers

Brown beef and drain. In large pot with lid add water, tomatoes, and Sloppy Joe Seasoning. Mix well, and bring to a boil. Then add Ramen noodles (broken up some), beef and bell pepper. Next reduce heat to simmer and cover with lid. Cook for 20-30 min. watching closely so that it doesn't stick or need more water added. This meal serves 6 people.

Beef Tomato Noodle Skillet

1 package of Ramen Noodles crunched up
2 cans of tomatoes
1 can of corn (not creamed)
1 lb ground beef

Directions

Brown the beef and drain. Add the tomatoes, corn, and noodles. Make sure to add the seasoning package to the meal. Bring to boil. Cover, stirring occasionally. Bring the meal until most of the tomato sauce is evaporated and the noodles are soft.

Breakfast Burritos With A Kick

2 cups water
1 pkg ramen noodles, any flavor you like
1 egg, beaten
1/4 cup shredded cheese
hot sauce- (We use Franks)
flour tortilla

Bring water to a boil, add ramen. While ramen is cooking slowly pour in beaten egg, add seasoning packet (Cook for 3 minutes). Drain, reserving about 1 T. of water. Add cheese & Hot Sauce (to taste preference). Fill a warm

flour tortilla, wrap and enjoy. This makes a fast, hearty breakfast on the go for 2 people.

Fajitas A Ramen

1 package chicken flavored Ramen noodles, cooked with spice pack and drained
1 lb boneless chicken breasts, cubed
1 lb bulk Italian sausage, either sweet or hot
1 large can stewed tomatoes
2 green peppers, sliced
2 red peppers, sliced
1 onion, sliced
1 packet of taco seasoning
red pepper flakes to taste
Salt to taste

Brown Italian sausage in large pot, breaking up into small pieces. When browned,
add chicken cubes and saute until done. Add tomatoes, taco seasoning, red pepper flakes, salt, and onion; cook until onion is soft. Add green and red peppers, cook until peppers are cooked and slightly soft. Toss with cooked Ramen noodles. Serve with a side of salsa, guacamole, and sour cream if desired.

Chicken Stroganoff On Ramen

1. Saute boneless chicken, cut into small bites (1.5 lb), chopped white onions (1/2 cup) and 1/2 lb chopped mushrooms (can use a can, drained in a pinch), and one tbsp. soy sauce. Add 1/2 tsp. each of garlic powder, sea salt, and pepper.
2. Prepare two packages of ramen noodles, chicken style but just use one seasoning packet.
3. Steam two small crowns of broccoli and cut off stems.
4. Drain noodles and broccoli, Add 1/2 container of low fat sour cream, and 1 tbsp. of chopped

chives. Mix all together, cover and let the ingredients blend for a few minutes.

Bacon % Chicken Ramen

1/2 onion
1 tablespoon olive oil
one clove of garlic
1 – 2 slices of bacon (depending on preference)
chicken slices (approx the size of your palm)
soy sauce
mixed vegetables
1 packet of whichever noodles you prefer, I use fresh noodles for simplicity (no need to boil them)

If you have noodles that need boiling, I would advise putting them on first. Next, slice the onion & shred the garlic or cut it up (finely). Cut up the bacon into small pieces & add all of the above into a wok (which already has a small amount of olive oil in it) on a low heat.

Get the chicken & cut it up, & add it to the wok. Cook until the chicken is completely cooked (a good sign of this is that it's completely changed color all over), then add the soy sauce. Allow to cook for a minute extra & then add the mixed vegetables & stir. Then add the cooked noodles, serve & enjoy.

Elegant Balsamic Ramen Chicken

3 medium-sized boneless skinless chicken breasts
4 bell peppers (I prefer one of each: red, orange, yellow, green), sliced
A hearty dish of Chicken in creamy balsamic sauce mingled with sweet onions and red, yellow and green bell peppers.
3 medium-sized boneless skinless chicken breasts
4 bell peppers (I prefer one of each: red, orange, yellow, green), sliced
2 medium sweet onions, sliced
1 tbsp butter
4 tbsp Extra Virgin Olive Oil (EVOO)
2 tbsp flour
1/4 cup balsamic vinegar
1/4 cup heavy cream
3 packages Ramen noodles
salt&pepper

Bring a large pot of salted water to a boil. Add ramen noodles and cook until al dente. (Do not add seasoning packet.)

Meanwhile, in a large skillet, heat half of the EVOO over medium heat. Season chicken with salt and pepper. Cooking time will depend on thickness of breasts. Remove from skillet and let rest on a cutting board. Add the rest of the EVOO and sautee onions and bell peppers for about 20 minutes, or until preferred texture. Add butter until melted, and whisk in flour. Add vinegar and cream. Stir together. Slice chicken into bite sized pieces and add to mixture. Drain pasta and add as well. Serve and enjoy!

Part 2

Ramen Burger

Ingredients:

Makes 3 burgers Servings

2 Packages of instant ramen noodles, flavor packet discarded

2 Large size eggs (Mid size will do.)

Salt and Pepper just for taste

3/4 pound lean ground beef (or ground beef.)

1-2 Tablespoons of soy sauce

1-2 Teaspoons of sesame oil

2-3 Tablespoons vegetable oil, divided

3 slices American cheese (or six slices for extra cheese.)

1/4 cup ketchup

2-3 tablespoons of chile-garlic sauce (I like Sriracha Hot Sauce.)

1-2 cups arugula

3 large eggs (set aside)

Directions

Start by boiling water in a pot; Now add your ramen noodles.

Boil, while stirring occasionally, or until noodles are nice and tender,

Cook this for about 3-4 minutes. Now drain everything. Allow your noodles to cool off.

Now beat 2 eggs in a bowl; You may season with salt and pepper if you like. Stir the noodles into your eggs or until bowl is coated. next go ahead and divide noodles into 4-6 burger-size rounds into bowls. Place a sheet of plastic wrap directly over noodles and stack bowls on top of each other to flatten out noodles.

Refrigerate the bowl until nice and firm, about 20-60 minutes.

While the noodles are cooling off mix ground beef, sesame oil, and soy sauce, in a bowl. Next divide beef mixture into patties. (about 4-6.)

Heat 1-2 tablespoons of vegetable oil, next place it into a large skillet set to medium-heat. Grab your cooled ramen and turn each ramen bowl over. Go ahead and gently tap bottom of the bowl. The ramen loosens, and carefully remove to maintain its bun shape.

Fry each ramen bun, (without moving noodles,) let it sit in oil until brown, do this for about 3 minutes.

Now flip each noodle bun, and fry the other side until crisp, 3 to 4 minutes more. Don't burn them (Noodles will look golden brown on each side.)

Should be crispy on one side, And softer on the other. move your noodle buns to large plate with crispy side up. (looking good so far!)

Heat up your 1-2 tablespoons of vegetable oil use the same skillet.(That you fried your ramen in.

Go ahead and start cooking up beef patties until burgers are cooked to liking.

Mix the ketchup in chile-garlic sauce in a small size bowl;

You may spread mixture on the crispy side of each ramen bun.

Next divide arugula over the ramen buns. Place burgers on top of arugula.

Heat about 1-2 teaspoons of oil in a skillet , fry the remaining eggs (one at a time.)

You can add a little more oil if needed, When yolk is almost firm, in about 1 minute or so per side. Place the egg over patty then add remaining noodle bun.

That's it your done enjoy!

Ramen Noodle Burger: Bok Choy

INGREDIENTS

1 packet Ramen noodles

2 eggs

7 oz. ground beef

2 scallions

A little soy sauce

Splash of sesame oil

1 head of bok choy

Tomato ketchup

A little hot sauce

Slice of American cheese (or what ever slice cheese.)

Splash of oil (For cooking.)

PREPARATION

Boil the noodles in a salted water bath according to instructions,

But don't add the seasoning packets. Drain all the water.

Now cook up your Ramen Buns, using the (EASY RAMEN BUNS method at the beginning of book.)

Next slice up the scallions then mix them into the beef, go ahead and add noodle seasoning, sesame oil, and soy sauce. Now form two burger patties, make them similar size as your buns, still keeping them pretty thin.

Heat up the three frying pans. Fry the burgers in one pan with a shot of oil for a minute or so on each side.

1. Remove the chilled ramen burger buns from the plastic wrap and fry in a shot of oil in the second pan for 2 minutes on each side so that they get golden and crispy.
2. Crack egg and fry in the third pan.
3. Mix together the ketchup and hot sauce.

Wash the bok choy then steam it very quickly in the pan (use only a dash of water.)

Drain everything place on paper towels to remove grease.

Ramen burger buns with a slices of cheese on top of each burger patty.

 Arrange them any way you see fit.

Homemade Ramen Burger 3 (Bacon Flavored)

Ingredients:

1 Pack of ramen noodles
1 egg any size
Burger ingredients:
Burger patty (frozen)
Curry powder (if you like)
Lettuce, Tomatoes, Spinach, etc
Bacon bits or any bacon flavored Onion Crunch
Cheese slice (optional)
Fried egg (To top)
1 teaspoon of butter

Directions:
START BY USING THE EASY RAMEN BUNS

Boil a pot of water. Add the noodles then the season packet. Cook the noodles until they are tender (but not too soft, cook for about 2 to 4 minutes. Now drain everything, and let cool down.

Now place the noodles in the bowl. Beat the eggs then pour it over the noodles, tossing it around to coat well.

Next divide the noodles into 2 plastic containers. Place them plastic wrap, (or baking parchment.)

Now place 1 container on top of the other.

Place 3rd container on top that stack.

Next place a weight such as a can of soup into the top container.

Place stack in refrigerator, and let chill about 1-2 hours.

Next heat up 2 tablespoons of oil (Use a nonstick skillet, set to medium heat.

Now carefully remove ramen buns.(CAREFULLY!) from containers and place them in oil. Fry them until they are light brown and nice and crisp.

Turn your buns (You may add a little oil if needed.) Fry them up until brown on other side. Remove and drain off on paper towels.

Start by heating up and/cooking your burger patty.

Make a free form patty with ground beef, curry powder and salt. To add more of a Japanese flare.

Heat your pan with a little oil and butter.

Flip over your ramen noodle container upside down so that the noodle bun slides easily into frying pan in one piece.

Fry for a few minutes on both sides until noodles become slightly crispy.

Add in patty and additional toppings of your choice.

RAMEN WAFFLE SANDWICH

The waffle will be soft inside with a little bit crunch along the edges.

Method:

Start by boiling the the ramen the usual way.

Drain . In a mixing bowl, whisk up 1 egg, 2 tablespoons white flour, 1/2 teaspoon baking powder, 2 tablespoons water, and 1/2 packet chicken flavoring.

Add the noodles and mix together. (Use your hands so you don't break them up.)

Now go ahead split the mixture in two sections into your waffle maker, and cook them on the darkest setting.

All done build your breakfast beast of a sandwich.

Ramen Turkey Burger 5

Ingredients

1 package ground turkey

1 tablespoon of soy sauce (Sub for teriyaki sauce if you like.)

1 tablespoon of minced garlic

1 tsp of chili pepper flakes

Salt and pepper just for taste

1 pack of ramen noodles (1 for each burger.)

2 eggs (1 per burger .)

Hot Sriracha sauce or (any hot sause.)

Arugula

Diced greed onion

Sautéd red onion, or any other onion rings

1 tablespoon oil or (sesame oil.)

Take the first 5 ingredients then mix them all together. (Use a small- mid bowl.)

Make about 4 turkey hamburger patties. (Use your hands to make rounds.)

Grill up and fry them as desired.

Cook your ramen noodles the normal way just leave out the flavor packet.

Next drain your noodles.

Whisk up the eggs then coat your noodles.

Now separate the noodles in half. Place one half in one ramekin dish, the other half in a second ramekin dish. Place saran wrap over each dish and press the noodles down with a can of food or another bowl. Refrigerate for about 10-15 minutes.

Make your sriracha sauce by using half sriracha per half ketchup. Stir it all up.

Now to make the "buns", carefully place the noodle cakes into a medium/hot pan. Fry until golden brown on both sides. You have just made your buns.

Fry the egg over easy or over medium.

Time to assemble the turkey burgers.

Spread some sriracha ketchup on the bottom half of your noodle bun. Place a nice layer of arugula, then add the turkey hamburger patty on top. Next, go ahead and your cheese slice, then the fried egg, and onions (sauté, green onions). All done enjoy.

Vegan Eggplant Burger

Ingredients
Ramen Noodle Buns

4 ounces of ramen noodles
2 flax eggs (2 tablespoons of ground flax seed)
2 tablespoons green onion, sliced thin
¼ teaspoon salt
¼ teaspoon ground black pepper
1 teaspoon extra-virgin olive oil (or more)

Eggplant Burger

1 medium eggplant, peeled and diced into small cubes (approximately 3-3½ cups)
⅓ cup finely chopped red pepper
1 cup vegan bread crumbs (or more)
1 flax egg (1 tablespoon of ground flax seed)
1 shallot, minced
1 garlic clove, minced
1 teaspoon fresh chopped rosemary (or ½ teaspoon dried)
¼ teaspoon coriander
½ teaspoon oregano

½ teaspoon salt
1 tablespoon fresh squeezed lemon juice
¼ teaspoon ground black pepper
2 tablespoons fresh parsley, chopped
2 teaspoons of extra-virgin olive oil

Tahini Sauce

⅛ cup lemon juice
½ cup tahini paste (sesame-seed paste)
1 garlic clove, minced
¼ teaspoon salt
Couple of twists of fresh ground black pepper

Instructions

Tahini Sauce

Combine all sauce ingredients into a bowl and whisk until smooth. If too thick, add a little warm water a teaspoon at a time until desired consistency. Refrigerate.

RAMEN BUNS

1 package of dry ramen noodles, any flavor, will do. (I like Top Ramen Noodles.)

1 egg (Small size egg will do.)

3 round plastic containers, (Have them at about 4 inches diameter.)

2-3 tablespoons of Vegetable oil

Boil a pot of water. Add the noodles then the season packet. Cook the noodles until they are tender (but not too soft, cook for about 2 to 4 minutes. Now drain everything, and let cool down.

Now place the noodles in the bowl. Beat the eggs then pour it over the noodles, tossing it around to coat well.

Next divide the noodles into 2 plastic containers. Place them plastic wrap, (or baking parchment.)

Now place 1 container on top of the other.

Place 3rd container on top that stack.

Next place a weight such as a can of soup into the top container.

Place stack in refrigerator, and let chill about 1-2 hours.

Next heat up 2 tablespoons of oil (Use a nonstick skillet, set to medium heat.

Now carefully remove ramen buns.(CAREFULLY!) from containers and place them in oil. Fry them until they are light brown and nice and crisp.

Turn your buns (You may add a little oil if needed.) Fry them up until brown on other side. Remove and drain off on paper towels. (One pack serves 1.)

Eggplant burger

Whisk together 1 tablespoon of ground flax seed and about 2-3 tablespoons of water. Refrigerate for the next 10 minutes or longer if needed.

Now grab a large non-stick skillet, lets heat up 1 teaspoon of oil set to medium-high heat. Add the eggplant cubes with red pepper. Saute them until the eggplant is brown nice and soft. (Add a little bit of vegetable broth if it starts to get sticky instead of adding more oil.)

Add the salt and pepper, shallot, rosemary, garlic, coriander and oregano. Cook for about 1-2 minutes. Taste and adjust your seasonings if needed.

Remove from pan and mash with a potato masher (If you have one) until completely crushed.

Add the bread crumbs to parsley , lemon juice, flax egg and combine them. (if needed add some more bread crumbs.)

Refrigerate covered for about 25-30 minutes or longer.

Heat oil set to medium-high heat in a large non-stick skillet .

(Get your hand wet so the mixture does not stick) Now useing your wet hands, divide up the eggplant mixture into about 4 burgers. Use your skillet to cook them until golden brown on each side.

Turn them very gently so they don't break.

Serve them on top of ramen noodle bun.

Drizzle with a little tahini sauce

Top the burgers with your favorite garnishes like: lettuce, tomatoes , vegan cheese, and red onion.

Here's a idea! Serve these little burgers in pita bread or lettuce wraps.

Ramen Hisago Burger

RAMEN BUNS

1 package of dry ramen noodles, any flavor, will do. (I like Top Ramen Noodles.)
1 egg (Small size egg will do.)
3 round plastic containers, (Have them at about 4 inches diameter.)
2-3 tablespoons of Vegetable oil

Boil a pot of water. Add the noodles then the season packet. Cook the noodles until they are tender (but not too soft, cook for about 2 to 4 minutes. Now drain everything, and let cool down.

Now place the noodles in the bowl. Beat the eggs then pour it over the noodles, tossing it around to coat well.
Next divide the noodles into 2 plastic containers. Place them plastic wrap, (or baking parchment.)
Now place 1 container on top of the other.
Place 3rd container on top that stack.
Next place a weight such as a can of soup into the top container.
Place stack in refrigerator, and let chill about 1-2 hours.

Next heat up 2 tablespoons of oil (Use a nonstick skillet, set to medium heat.

Now carefully remove ramen buns.(CAREFULLY!) from containers and place them in oil. Fry them until they are light brown and nice and crisp.

Turn your buns (You may add a little oil if needed.) Fry them up until brown on other side. Remove and drain off on paper towels. (One pack serves 1.)

Hisago Burger

1-1/2 tablespoons dehydrated onion
1/2 cup hot water
4 slices white bread, torn in pieces
2 pounds ground beef (80 percent lean)
1-1/2 tablespoons minced celery
1/4 teaspoon salt, or to taste
1/4 teaspoon pepper, or to taste
1 teaspoon vegetable oil

Cooking Process:

EASY RAMEN BUNS

1 package of dry ramen noodles, any flavor, will do. (I like Top Ramen Noodles.)
1 egg (Small size egg will do.)
3 round plastic containers, (Have them at about 4 inches diameter.)
2-3 tablespoons of Vegetable oil

Boil a pot of water. Add the noodles then the season packet. Cook the noodles until they are tender (but not too soft, cook for about 2 to 4 minutes. Now drain everything, and let cool down.

Now place the noodles in the bowl. Beat the eggs then pour it over the noodles, tossing it around to coat well.

Next divide the noodles into 2 plastic containers. Place them plastic wrap, (or baking parchment.)

Now place 1 container on top of the other.

Place 3rd container on top that stack.

Next place a weight such as a can of soup into the top container.

Place stack in refrigerator, and let chill about 1-2 hours.

Next heat up 2 tablespoons of oil (Use a nonstick skillet, set to medium heat.

Now carefully remove ramen buns.(CAREFULLY!) from containers and place them in oil. Fry them until they are light brown and nice and crisp.

Turn your buns (You may add a little oil if needed.) Fry them up until brown on other side. Remove and drain off on paper towels. (One pack serves 1.)

Hisago Delicatessen Burger

Soak onion in hot water until soft. Pour mixture over bread pieces and toss until bread falls apart and forms a soft paste (add more water if needed). Add beef, celery, salt and pepper; toss lightly to combine.

Form into 8 patties about 1 inch thick.

Here's a tip make a little depression in the center (This will help the burgers cook evenly).

Now put a little oil in skillet.

Fry the burgers set to medium-high heat cook them for about 5 minutes on each side.

If you would like to make sandwiches use: kalua pork, boneless teriyaki chicken, teriyaki hamburger patty (make sure it pre-cooked), 1 piece bulgogi, sliced up.

For the garnish add grilled onions, chopped green onion, arugula, BBQ sauce. All done enjoy!

Broccoli And Ramen Noodle Salad

Ingredients:

1 package broccoli coleslaw mix (16-24 ounce)
2 packages of chicken flavored ramen noodles
1 bunch green onions, chopped
1 cup unsalted peanuts
1 cup sunflower seeds (No shells)
1/4 cup white sugar
1/4 cup vegetable oil
1/3 cup apple cider vinegar

Directions

Break up ad cook noodles, drain all the water.

Use a large salad bowl, and combine the slaw with green onions.

Now add the broken noodles.

 Whisk everything together: sugar, oil, vinegar and the two ramen chicken seasoning packets. Now pour over salad and toss to evenly coat. Refrigerate until cool; next top with peanuts and sunflower seeds before serving. All done!

Asian Noodles"N Shrimp

Ingredients

1 can lite coconut milk

2 cup of preshredded carrots

1 medium size onion, (make sure you slice thinly.)

12 ounce raw medium shrimp, peeled and deveined

2 package shrimp-flavor ramen noodles (Set 1 seasoning pkt aside until needed.)

2 cups of snow peas, (Make sure strings are removed)

1/4 cup of finely chopped cilantro

3 teaspoons of fresh lime juice

Directions

Bring two 1/4 cups of water, add the coconut milk, carrots and onion to a boil (Use 10 inch skillet is best.)

Next grab your snow peas, ramen noodles and shrimp; (press them down to submerge in juices.) Bring everything to a nice simmer and, stirring to break up noodles, simmer for about 2 to 4 minutes more or until shrimp are cooked through.

Remove from heat and stir in that extra seasoning packet, add cilantro and lime juice for taste. Now serve immediately.

Coconut Curry Shrimp

Ingredients

2 package ramen noodles (Any flavor will do but Shrimp is best)

1/2 cup light coconut milk

1/3 cup creamy peanut butter (Try nutty peanut butter for a extra crunch.)

2 tablespoons of fresh lime juice

1/4 teaspoon of crushed red pepper flakes (optional)

1 pound of cooked, large shrimp, cleaned, peeled (thawed out not frozen.)

1/2 cucumber, cut into thin half moon sizes

4 scallions, sliced diagonally or what ever way you like

4 Lime wedges, (Just for serving.)

Directions

Boil up 4 cups of water (large skillet is best.) Break each package of noodles into 4 sections if you can. Now add to boiling water (save the seasoning packets use them for something else). Cover skillet with lid, next remove from heat and sit for about 5 minutes.

While that's sitting, in a Mid-large bowl, whisk the lime juice , peanut butter, coconut milk, and red pepper.

Now drain the noodles. Add everything together into the bowl with the dressing.

After that add cucumber, shrimp, and scallions toss it up. Serve with a side of lime wedges.

Ramen'n Beef or Chicken with Veggies

4 packs of Ramen, (You may use any flavor.)

1 pound of Chicken or Beef. (If you use Tofu, make sure it serves 4 people.)

1 Cup Frozen Veggies, (Its your choice, anything you have.)

You may add shredded Cheese if you desire.

Sauté your meat or meats until done.

Next cook Ramen in just enough water to cover noodles. Now add frozen veggies to Ramen cook for 1 minute just before noodles are done.

Drain some of the water when Ramen is done,

The noodles should be a chunky soup, (a lot of water.) Then add flavoring packs, Place in large bowl, top with shredded cheese, if you want. You may serve with a side of bread.

All Done Enjoy!

Easy Noodle Salad

Ingredients:

Servings: 4-6 people
1 bag coleslaw mix about 16oz
1 package ramen noodles, raw & crushed (Any flavor)
1/2 cup sunflower seeds (no shells.)
1/2 cup oil (olive is best)
1/4 cup Apple cider vinegar
1/4 cup sugar (Sub for 6 packs of Splenda.)

Directions:

1. Mix together the coleslaw mix, crushed noodles& sunflower kernels.
2. In a small- mid size bowl, mix the Ramen Noodle seasoning packs.

3. Next add,oil, vinegar& sugar together.

4. Mix everything together and refrigerate at least 1-2 hours

5. All done! How easy was that?

Ramen Noodle Casserole

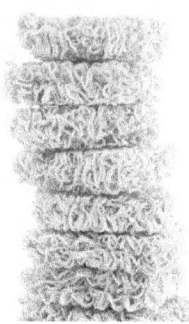

Ingredients

1 lb ground chuck

1 small -medium size onion , (Diced up.)

1 cup of diced tomatoes

3 packages beef-flavor ramen noodles

2-3 cups water

You may add Velveeta cheese, just for taste.

Instructions

Cook the Hamburger and onion until brown , Next add your 3 flavoring packets and simmer for about 4 minutes.

Add a 1/2cup water + tomatoes and bring them both to a boil.

Next add your noodles and cook them for about 3-4 minutes longer.

After that pour into a casserole dish,(make sure you spray it with cooking spray.) Now cover with sliced Velveeta cheese or any cheese you have.

Place it in the oven and bake for 15 minutes set to 325-350°

When cheese is melted your done. That's it enjoy!

Grilled Ramen

1 tbs Rice wine vinegar

2 tbs of Sesame oil

Take a ramen block, marinate it for about 20 minutes in things like rice wine vinegar and sesame oil, then grill it for 3 minutes on each side.

You may serve it alone, or add in some grilled vegetables.

Taking your BBQ to a whole new level.

Cheesy Baked Ramen (macaroni and cheese of ramen)

Boxed macaroni and cheese (Powder or Packed cheese)

If you don't have that use cheese-in-a-can

Shredded Cheese

Boil your Ramen to taste, next just add boxed cheese while Noodles are still warm.

Add in a little butter if your noodles start to stick. Mix everything up and top with Shredded Cheese. That's it!

Ramen Spam/ Ham

Ingredients:

2 packages of chicken ramen noodles, (Make sure you break them up up slightly)

3-4 cups of water

1 can of spam,or canned ham (Diced them up in small cubes)

1/4 cup of green peas

1/4 cup of green onions, (slice them up)

1 teaspoon garlic powder or 1/4 teaspoon of garlic salt

1 tablespoon sesame oil

In a medium size pan, boil over set to high heat.

Next add the two packages of ramen noodles, and peas.

Cook for about 2-3 minutes, Now drain everything.

Now while noodles are cooking, heat up the sesame oil (use a small frying pan), add in spam cubes and green onion, stirring everything up occasionally to brown up the cubes.

After they are nice and browned add everything to the frying pan,

Next add the two seasoning packets, garlic powder or garlic salt, Start mixing well. That's it your ready to serve!

Chicken Broccoli Noodles

2 pkgs. (3 oz. each) Ramen Pride chicken flavor Ramen noodle soup

1 can (10 3/4 oz.) Campbell's condensed cream of mushroom soup

1/2 soup can milk

1 c. cubed cooked chicken

1 c. cooked broccoli flowerets

Prepare Ramen noodle soup according to package directions. Add seasoning packets; drain most of the liquid. Stir in mushroom soup and milk. Add chicken and broccoli. Heat through. Makes 5 1/2 cups.

MARINATED NOODLES AND CABBAGE

1 (3 oz.) pkg. Oriental noodles with chicken flavor, like Top Ramen

1/4 cup oil

3 tbsp. rice vinegar

1 tbsp. sugar

1/4 tsp. salt

2 cup finely shredded cabbage

1 (6 3/4 oz.) can chunk-style chicken, drained

1/4 cup sliced green onion

3 tbsp. fried sesame seed

3 tbsp. sliced almonds, toasted

Green pepper cut into rings

Break the noodles up.

In a mixing bowl combine the ramen seasoning packet then mix with vinegar, oil, sugar, 1/4 teaspoon salt and dash of pepper.

Stir to dissolve up all the seasonings.

Stir in broken noodles, cabbage, chicken, onion and sesame seed.

Cover it up.

Chill it for a few hours. Now before you start serving stir in the almonds, and garnish it off with some green peppers rings. Looks so nice and taste so good!

Top Ramen Noodle Cole Slaw

4 tbsp. sugar
2 tsp. salt
1 tsp. pepper
1/3 c. vinegar
2/3 c. Miracle Whip
1 med. head cabbage
5 green onions (optional)
8 tbsp. slivered almonds, toasted
8 tbsp. sesame seeds, toasted
1 can crushed pineapple, drained
Top Ramen noodles, broken
Seasonings from noodles

Prepare the dressing ahead of time and refrigerate over night.

Next mix up sugar, pepper, salt, vinegar and seasoning on top of the noodles,

Heat everything until sugar dissolves. Let it sit for a while until nice and cool.

Next add Miracle Whip and mix up well. Refrigerate for about 1-2 hours.

Shred some cabbage up fine, then add onions.

Good ahead and add your dressing, .

The last thing you need to do is add the broken noodles, almonds, sesame seeds, and pineapple.

Serves 10 to 12 people. (WOW!)

RAMEN NOODLE TACOS(YES TACOS!!!)

2 pkg. of Beef Ramen noodles or (any brand)

1 lb. Ground Beef or Ground Chicken / Turkey

1/2 head of Lettuce - Chopped up into fine slices

Cheese - (Shredded 3 cheese taco mix is best)

2 Tomatoes

Any other taco toppings you want to add

Taco shells

Taco sauce

Taco season pack.

Cook the noodles normal according to package ,

Don't add beef seasoning packets to noodles.(Place them aside)

Cook ground beef until nice and Brown. When done drain the juices.

Go ahead and grab the 2 beef packs and mix with beef. You may top with cheese at this time if you like. Drain noodles.

To make tacos:

Place the cut lettuce on serving plate.

Layer noodles on bottom of shell, then add beef.

Add any other taco toppings on top.

ALL DONE THAT"S IT!

EASY ORIENTAL NOODLE SALAD

1 head of cabbage shredded (or buy per packed shredded cabbage.)

6 scallions

1 1/2 cup. toasted almond slivers

4 tablespoon. sesame seeds (You may roast them at 350 degrees for about 4-5 minutes)

2 package of Ramen noodles (Make sure you crush them up)

Blend everything the ingredients and the dressing.

Now let's make the DRESSING:

2/3 oil

5 tablespoon. Apple cider vinegar or reg vinegar will do

3/4 tsp. salt

3/4 tsp. pepper

2 pkgs flavor packs from noodles

1 tablespoon. sugar or sugar sub

Mix everything up and now you have a nice dressing.

Sesame-Noodle Shrimp Salad

1/3 cup rice vinegar

1/4 cup vegetable oil

2 tablespoon. sugar

1 garlic clove, minced up very fine

1/2 teaspoon. salt

2 teaspoon. soy sauce (any brand will do!)

1 teaspoon of sesame seed oil

1 teaspoon. hot chili paste (If you want)

1 teaspoon. sesame seeds, (Best if toasted)

SALAD:

2 pkgs. Ramen (Any flavor,)

1/2 lb. cooked lg. shrimp, peeled, and deveined (Save money by using salad shrimp)

2 cup finely shredded purple cabbage

2-3 thin green onions, smashed flat then shredded

1/3 cup slivered almonds, toasted

2-3 tbsp. fresh coriander leaves, shredded

Prepare dressing by mixing together all ingredients - then set aside.

Japan Like A Pro

Ingredients

Noodles

9 oz fresh angel hair pasta or 1 Ramen pack

8 cups water (2L)

2 Tbsp baking soda

Salted pork

1 lb pork

1 tsp salt

Soup

5-6 cups water

50grams of ginger root, (Make sure its sliced up good)

2-3 cloves garlic, (Cut and skinned)

1 Bunch green onions

4 Tablespoons soy sauce

2 Tablespoons sake

1 teaspoon salt

1 teaspoon sesame oil

Topping

Boiled a few egg halves

Bean sprouts, Have them blanched briefly

Green onions, cut them up finely

Instructions

Start by rubbing salt on the pork, Now it let it sit overnight placed in the fridge.

In a pot, put water, ginger root, garlic, green onions and salted pork, and boil set to high heat.

Make sure you Skim the fat, and any floating crap.

Next cover it up, and reduce to low heat, and simmer this for about 1 - 2 hours.

When ready let the broth pork cool down completely. (Let it rest in the pot)

Strain the pot, and remove pork.

Slice the pork, now set it aside for a topping later on.

Moving on get ready to prepare the rest of the toppings as well add the.

(blanched bean sprouts, boiled eggs, cut green onions), Do this before making soup and noodles.

Once the noodles are cooked, you will need to add your soup and toppings right away. (If you wait to long the noodles will get soft.) Then game over! If this happens grab a fresh pack and start cooking them over.

Boil the broth and adding soy sauce, salt, sake, and sesame oil.

Let it simmer set to low heat until noodles are ready.

Don't worry the next part is easy!

Now in a boiling pot of water, (Keep a eye on it, may boil over), then add the Ramen. Cook your pasta for 30 seconds, and strain.

Next Quickly divide noodles into bowls.

Now add the soup onto noodles. Top with bean sprouts, boiled eggs, green onions and sliced pork. ALL DONE!

The Greatest Ever Juicy Juice Burger

INGREDIENTS

1/4 cup Mayonnaise
1/2 cup plain dry bread crumbs
1 Onion Soup Mix
2 lbs. ground beef [or ground turkey]
1/2 cup finely chopped red onion
8 hamburger buns

Directions

Go ahead ,and combine the Mayonnaise, bread crumbs ,and Soup Mix in bowl.

mix up the mayonnaise mixture into ground beef; shape into 8 patties.

GRILL or broil until done. Serve burgers on buns.

The faster you eat, the faster you could grab another.

The SPIKE BURGER

INGREDIENTS

1 & 1/2 pound Ground Beef [or ground turkey]

1/4 cup finely chopped red onion

4 of tablespoons barbecue sauce

4 slices white Cheddar with pepper Jack ,and smoked Gouda or try provolone cheese

4 whole wheat hamburger buns or any rolls, split, (toasted)

Lettuce leaves, tomato slices ,and red onion slices

Lets Grill

Combine the Ground Beef, onion ,and 2 tablespoons barbecue sauce in medium bowl,mixing lightly but thoroughly. Shape them into four 1/2-inch thick patties.

Place patties on grid with medium heat, ash-covered coals. Grill, covered, 8 to 10 minutes (over medium heat on preheated your grill, for 8 - 10 minutes) or until instant-read thermometer inserted horizontally into center registers 160°F, turning occasionally. About 1 minute before burgers are done, you may brush on 2 tablespoons barbecue sauce ,then top with cheese.

Line bottom half of each bun with lettuce leaves, tomato ,and red onion slices, as desired; top with burger. Then Close s,andwiches. All done take big bites filling your mouth let the barbecue sauce drip down your shirt.

Grilled T-Bone Steaks With Rub A Dub

INGREDIENTS

2 to 6 beef T-Bone or Porterhouse Steaks, cut each one 1 inch thick
Pinch of Salt for each

BBQ Rub a dub:

2 tablespoons chili powder
3 tablespoons packed brown sugar
1 tablespoon ground cumin
2 teaspoons minced garlic
2 teaspoons cider vinegar
1 teaspoon Worcestershire sauce
1/4 teaspoon ground red pepper

Combine some BBQ Rub ingredients ,and press evenly onto beef steaks.

Place steaks on metal grid with medium, ash-covered coals. Grill, covered, 8 to 14 minutes (over medium heat on preheated gas grill, 8 to 10 minutes) for medium rare (145°F) to medium (160°F) doneness, turning occasionally. Remove bones ,and carve steaks into slices, if desired. Season with salt, as needed. Stack all the removed bones into a bowl ,and suck off any remaining meat. Lets not let any meat get away from our stomach.

The Whole Damn Chicken

INGREDIENTS:
2 whole chickens (about 3 lb. each)
2 small lemons, cut them in half
1 cup Baby Ray Original Barbecue Sauce
1 tsp. Italian seasoning
4 cloves garlic, peeled

Let's Grill

Start off by heating grill for indirect grilling. Light one side of the grill, while leaving other side unlit. Close lid; heat grill between 300-350ºF.

TRIM ,and discard excess any fat from the chickens. Squeeze lemon juice into small bowl reserve lemon halves. Add some barbecue sauce, ,and seasoning to juice; mix well. Place the 2 lemon halves ,and garlic cloves inside each chicken cavity. Take 1 minute, ,,,and down a beer. Don't talk to anyone now crush the empty beer can the get back to work. Place the chickens breast sides up, over grate over unlit area then cover. Grill for about 1 &1/2 to 2 hours or, until chicken is done 165°F, turning ,and brushing occasionally with sauce for the last 18-20 min. Remove ,and discard lemon halves ,and garlic from chickens before serving. Chickens don't fly for a reason.

2) Beef Stew

A comforting food for cold winters

Cooking Time: **10 minutes**

Makes: 8 servings

List of Ingredients:

- 2 ½ lb. beef meant for stewing
- 1can of stewed tomatoes
- 1 cup celery, chopped
- 3 medium potatoes, cubed
- 4 medium carrots, sliced
- 3 onions, chopped
- 2 cubes of beef bouillon
- 3 ½ tablespoons of tapioca
- 1/8 teaspoons each of dried marjoram, thyme and rosemary
- ¼ cup of red wine
- 10 oz. frozen peas

Procedure:

1. Preheat your Dutch oven at 250 degrees.
2. Place everything except in your preheated oven and cover.
3. Let it cook for 5-6 hours.
4. Add in the peas before the last half hour.

3) Lamb Stew

A hearty dish that tastes of Greece all the way

Cooking Time: **15 minutes**

Makes: 4 servings

List of Ingredients:
- 1 lb. lamb shoulder chops
- 1 cup of lamb stock
- 2 tablespoons of olive oil
- Salt and black pepper to taste
- 1 onion, finely chopped
- 3 cloves of garlic, minced
- 2 cups of tomatoes, chopped
- 15 oz. canned tomato sauce
- ½ cup of dry red wine
- Juice and zest of half lemon
- ½ teaspoons each of ground cinnamon and oregano
- 1 lb. fresh green beans, cleaned
- 1 bay leaf
- ¼ cup of parsley, chopped

Procedure:

1. Heat the oil in the Dutch oven.
2. After seasoning the lamb blade chops, add them to the oven on high heat and brown them on all sides.

3. Add the onions and garlic and cook for another 2 minutes.

4. Pour in the wine. Let it boil then turn down heat to simmer.

5. Add in the stock, tomato sauce, tomatoes, lemon juice and zest, cinnamon, bay leaf and oregano.

6. When it comes to simmering again, cover and let it cook for an hour and a half or until lamb is tender.

7. Stir in green beans and cook for 20 more minutes.

8. Remove bones and bay leaf.

9. Serve, garnished with parsley.

4) Chicken Gumbo

A traditional dish that can be easily made using a Dutch oven

Cooking Time: **20 minutes**

Makes: 2-4 servings

List of Ingredients:
- 2 lb. boneless, cubed chicken breasts
- 3 medium tomatoes, chopped
- 2 onions, chopped
- 2 celery sticks, chopped
- 2 bell peppers, chopped
- 2 lb. okra, sliced into ¼ inches
- 2 cloves of garlic minced
- 3 tablespoons of plain flour
- 4 tablespoons vegetable cooking oil
- Salt and pepper to taste

Procedure:

1. Bring the temperature to 325 degrees, or adjust it to 'Frying'.
2. Heat up the oil and add flour.
3. Keep stirring until golden.
4. Add onion, garlic and peppers and stir for a minute.
5. Add a quart of water with seasonings.

6. Add the vegetables and let it come to a boil.

7. Now reduce temperature to 225 and let it simmer, covered, for half an hour.

8. Add chicken cubes and simmer for another 20 minutes.

5) Baked Cauliflower With Cheese

Try this comforting baked cauliflower with cheese that will satiate most of your senses.

Cooking Time: **20 minutes**

Makes: 4 servings

List of Ingredients:
- 1 cauliflower head, cut into small florets
- 1/3 cup of chicken broth
- ½ cup of heavy cream
- Salt and black pepper to taste
- 1 tablespoon of flour
- 1 teaspoon mustard powder
- 2 tablespoons softened butter, divided
- 2 cloves of garlic, minced and divided
- ½ cup +1 tablespoon each of shredded cheddar and Monterrey Jack cheese
- ½ cup of bread crumbs
- ½ teaspoons of dried thyme

Procedure:

1. Mix together 1 tablespoon each of melted butter, both cheeses, half of garlic, a little bit of the seasonings with the bread crumbs and set it aside.

2. Add the remaining butter with garlic and flour in the Dutch oven. Cook for a minute.

3. Slowly pour in the broth and the cream and whisk to avoid lumps.

4. Add the rest of the seasonings and herbs and let it simmer (covered) for around 8 minutes or until the florets are tenderized.

5. Take it off the heat and then add the remaining cheeses.

6. Lastly top it with the bread crumb mixture and bake it at 450 degrees till the topping is nicely crisp and golden.

6) Fried And Succulent Chicken Wings

Who said you can only make stews and gravies in Dutch oven?

Cooking Time: **10 minutes**

Makes: 4 servings

List of Ingredients:

- 2 lb. chicken wings with skin
- Salt and pepper to taste
- ¼ cup plus 2 tablespoons sugar
- ½ cup of soy sauce
- Sprinkling of white sesame seeds
- Oil for deep frying

Procedure:

1. Use the oven's temperature to bring the oil to 300 degrees.

2. Season the chicken with salt and pepper.

3. Fry the wings for only 2-3 minutes in batches and take out on absorbent kitchen paper.

4. Re-fry the wings now on 350 degrees until they crisp up and are a nice golden brown colour.

5. Add soy sauce and sugar to a pan and bring it to a boil.

6. Let it simmer and wait till it has reduced nicely to a thick and sticky sauce.

7. Take off heat. Add the wings and sesame seeds to it.

8. Toss and take out to serve right away.

7) Chunky And Homey Chicken And Noodle Soup

A satisfying meal even for the most picky eaters
Cooking Time: **10 minutes**
Makes: 6 servings
List of Ingredients:
- 2 chicken breasts, boiled and shredded
- 48 oz. of chicken broth
- 1 teaspoon of hot sauce
- 1 tablespoon of Dijon mustard
- 5 garlic cloves, minced
- 3 tablespoons of olive oil
- 1 onion, chopped
- 5 fresh stalks of celery, chopped
- 1 cup of red peppers, chopped
- 4 carrots, sliced thinly
- 1 zucchini and yellow squash chopped into half inch pieces
- 1 ½ cup of eggplant, cut into half inch pieces
- 1 cup of parsley, chopped

Procedure:
1. Heat the oil in the Dutch oven.

2. Add onion and other vegetables. Stir while cooking until tender.

3. Add the garlic and stir in with the vegetables before pouring in the broth.

4. Let the soup come to a boil, then add the uncooked noodles.

5. Cook only until the noodles are perfectly done.

6. Add mustard, seasonings, chicken, hot sauce and parsley.

7. Reduce the heat and let it simmer for 5-10 minutes before serving so that everything comes together.

8) Chicken Pot Pie

An easy way to make something attractive and delicious

Cooking Time: **20 minutes**

Makes: 6 servings

List of Ingredients:

Besides all the ingredients that are required for the plain bread, you will need

- 1 – 1½ lb. chicken breast boneless, diced
- 1 onion, diced
- 4 potatoes, diced
- ¼ cup of plain flour
- ¾ cup of milk
- 1 lb. mixed (diced) vegetables
- 2 teaspoons poultry seasoning (any good brand)
- 2 teaspoons of garlic, minced
- 4 tablespoons oil
- 1 tube of refrigerated crescent rolls

Procedure:

1. Adjust the heat to 'Stewing' or 375 degrees.
2. Add oil to the oven.
3. Add garlic and chicken and stir until the chicken is done.

4. Add the onion and the potato to the oven and let it cook for 10 more minutes. Add the rest of the vegetables and seasonings.

5. Mix flour into the milk in a bowl.

6. Add the mixture to the pot and stir to get it incorporated.

7. When the mixture comes a boil, unroll the crescent rolls and create its layer on top of the chicken in the pot.

8. Cover and let the whole thing bake for 20 minutes at 350 degrees or until browned.

9) Chicken Coated With Herbs And Served With Orzo

The perfect dish if you can't think of anything else

Cooking Time: **10 minutes**

Makes: 6 servings

List of Ingredients:
- 8 oz. uncooked orzo pasta
- 2 breasts of chicken, halved lengthwise
- Salt and black pepper to taste
- 2 teaspoons of herb de Provence
- 2 tablespoons of olive oil
- 2 cloves of garlic, minced
- 1 shallot, chopped finely
- 1 can (14 oz.) of diced tomatoes, undrained
- 2 cups of broccoli florets
- ½ cup of heavy cream
- 1/3 cup of Parmesan cheese, grated

Procedure:

1. Cook the pasta according to directions given on package.

2. Season the chicken and then rub the herbs on both sides of all four chicken breast pieces.

3. Heat oil in the Dutch oven and sear the chicken from both sides.

4. Reduce heat and add shallot.

5. Keep stirring until sautéed.

6. Add garlic, stir and then add tomatoes and broccoli.

7. Let the mixture come to a boil and then reduce it to simmer.

8. Cover and cook for 15 minutes until the florets are crisp but tender.

9. In the end add in the pasta, cream and cheese.

10. Mix to incorporate.

10) Chicken And Dumplings

Go Chinese tonight!

Cooking Time: **5 minutes**

Makes: 3-4 servings

List of Ingredients:

- 1 can (12 oz.) of prepared chicken meat
- Buttermilk biscuit mix
- 2 large packets of chicken noodle soup mix

Procedure:

1. Adjust the temperature to 250 degrees for 'Stewing'.

2. Mix soup with half the amount of water specified. Add this mix and the chicken to the oven and let it come to a boil.

3. Meanwhile mix the biscuit mix and drop little spoonfuls into the soup.

4. Cover and bake the dish for about 30 minutes at 350 degrees.

11) Creamy Chicken Sauce For Pasta

You will be amazed at how easy, quick and tasty this dish is.

Cooking Time: **10 minutes**

Makes: 6 servings

List of Ingredients:

- 4 chicken breasts, skinless and boneless, cubed
- 6 bacon sliced, chopped
- 2 tablespoons readymade ranch salad dressing mix
- 3 cups uncooked pasta (any shape)
- 1 ¼ cups of milk
- 2 tablespoons of flour
- 1 tablespoon Parmesan cheese, shredded
- 2 tablespoons oil

Procedure:

1. Prepare the pasta according to the instructions given on its package.

2. Cook bacon in the Dutch oven until it goes crisp.

3. Take out the bacon on towel paper and also drain out all the fat leaving behind almost 2 tablespoons

4. Now add the chicken to the Dutch oven and cook until it becomes white all over.

5. Add flour and the dry salad mix and stir to thoroughly coat the chicken.

6. Before the flour starts to burn, add the milk.

7. Let it cook until it starts to reduce and seems thick and bubbly.

8. Return the bacon back to the oven and stir for a minute.

9. Serve chicken sauce over pasta in a platter and sprinkle cheese on top.

12) Chicken Cacciatore

A simple Italian dish that can be easily made using your Dutch oven

Cooking Time: **20 minutes**

Makes: 6 servings

List of Ingredients:
- 1 chicken cut in four pcs.
- 1onion, sliced
- 2 tablespoons of olive oil
- A pinch of salt and pepper each
- 8 oz. mushrooms, quartered
- 4 cloves of garlic, sliced
- 3 sprigs of rosemary,
- 1 cup of tomato sauce
- ½ cup of tomato sauce
- 1 teaspoon of dried oregano
- ½ cup of water
- ½ teaspoons of red chili flakes
- 2 each of red and green bell peppers
- Salt and pepper to taste

Procedure:

1. Preheat your Dutch oven to 350 degrees.

2. Add oil to the oven and let it heat up before adding chicken.

3. Let the chicken get brown and then remove to a mixing bowl.

4. Now add the onions and mushrooms and cook them while stirring until they become soft.

5. Add salt, pepper, red chilli flakes, garlic, rosemary, tomato sauce, oregano and water.

6. Place the chicken back into the Dutch oven over the veggies.

7. Add more salt if needed and lastly top with pepper slices.

8. Let it cook covered for 1hour and 15 minutes.

13) Baked Beans

This can be a wonderful treat for those who love pear.

Cooking Time: 20 minutes

Makes: 12 servings

List of Ingredients:

- 1 can (15 oz.) each of black beans, lima beans and kidney beans (rinsed and drained)
- 4 cans (15 oz. each) of pork and beans
- 1 bottle (18 oz.) barbeque sauce (honey flavored)
- 1 lb. ground beef
- ¾ lb. bacon
- 2 onions, chopped finely
- 3 tablespoons cider vinegar
- ½ cup of packed brown sugar
- Salt and pepper to taste

Procedure:

1. Preheat oven at 350 degrees.
2. Brown and crisp the bacon slices in a skillet and take out.
3. Now add the ground beef with onions in the skillet and cook until excess water has evaporated.
4. Transfer this mixture along with the bacon in the Dutch oven and add the rest of the ingredients.

5. Cover the pot and bake for an hour.

14) Chicken Fricassee

Beautifully aromatic French stew of chicken with vegetables

Cooking Time: 30 minutes

Makes: 6 servings

List of Ingredients:
- 2 ½ lb. chicken cut into 6-8 pcs.
- 1 ½ cups of chicken broth
- Salt and pepper to taste
- 2 tablespoons of flour
- 1 tablespoon of olive oil
- 5 shallots, finely chopped
- 1 cup of dry wine
- 1 medium carrot, sliced thinly after peeling
- 1lb of mushrooms, quartered
- 4 sprigs of tarragon
- 4 teaspoons of chopped fresh tarragon
- 1 tablespoon of cornstarch in 1 tablespoon of water
- 2 teaspoons of Dijon mustard
- ¼ cup of sour cream

Procedure:

1. Season your chicken pieces with salt, pepper and then coat with flour.

2. Heat the oil in Dutch oven and then add chicken for browning. Take out when done.

3. Add shallots and cook them for half a minute.

4. Add wine and simmer for three minutes.

5. Add the broth and wait till it starts to simmer then add the chicken with veggies and sprigs.

6. Cover and cook for 20 minutes.

7. Take out chicken and thrown sprigs.

8. Let the sauce reduce. Help it in thickening by adding cornstarch slurry.

9. In the end add mustard, sour cream and chopped tarragon.

15) Lentils In Honey

Honey gives a sweet little twist to an otherwise savory dish

Cooking Time: **10 minutes**

Makes: 8 servings

List of Ingredients:
- 1 lb. dry lentils
- 1 tablespoon soy sauce
- 1 bay leaf
- 3 cups of water
- 2 cans (14.5 oz. each) of chicken broth
- 2 teaspoons of salt
- 1 teaspoon dry mustard
- ¼ teaspoons of ground ginger
- ½ cup of honey
- ½ cup onion, chopped

Procedure:

1. Pour 2 cups of water, broth, salt and bay leaf in the Dutch oven and bring it to a boil.
2. Add the lentils and let it simmer for half an hour.
3. Take out the bay leaf and discard.
4. Preheat the oven to 350 degrees.

5. Add in the onion, ginger, soy sauce, mustard and remaining water in the pot.

6. Also drizzle honey on top of everything.

7. Cover and bake for around an hour or until lentils are done.

16) Crispy Fried Buttermilk Chicken

Have this retake of Southern fried chicken in your Dutch oven

Cooking Time: **10 minutes**

Makes: 4 servings

List of Ingredients:

- 3 ½ lb. chicken cut in 8 pcs
- 1 teaspoon each of salt, black pepper and paprika
- ¼ teaspoons each of dried oregano, dried rosemary, dried sage, cayenne pepper and ground thyme
- 2 cups of buttermilk.
- For Flour Coating
- 2 cups of flour
- 1 teaspoon of salt
- ½ teaspoons each of white pepper, onion powder, garlic powder, cayenne pepper and paprika
- 2 ½ quarts of peanut oil

Procedure:

1. Marinate the pieces of chicken in all of the spices.
2. Coat in buttermilk and keep refrigerated for 6 hours.
3. Add the seasonings to the flour and mix well.
4. Take chicken out of buttermilk and thoroughly coat each piece with flour.

5. Heat the oil in the Dutch oven up to 350 degrees.

6. Dust off excess flour and deep fry pcs for 10 minutes on each side.

7. Transfer to a cooling rack.

17) Cranberry And Bison Stew

A hearty winter dish that is both fulfilling and delicious

Cooking Time: **30 minutes**

Makes: 8 servings

List of Ingredients:
- 2 lb. Bison chuck roast, cubed
- 3 tablespoons oil
- 2 cans (14.5 oz. each) beef broth
- ½ cup of flour
- 2 cups of cranberry juice
- 1 ½ cups of fresh cranberries
- 1 teaspoon each of salt, dried marjoram and dried thyme
- 1 tablespoon of sugar
- ½ teaspoons of pepper
- 1 cup celery, sliced
- 2 cups of frozen green beans
- 1 ½ cups carrots, chopped

Procedure:

1. Coat the meat cubes with ¼ cup of flour, reserving the rest.
2. Heat oil in the Dutch oven and fry the meat cubes until browned from all sides.

3. Drain off the fat and add 3 cups of broth, cranberry juice, fresh cranberries, sugar, salt, pepper, onion, marjoram and thyme.

4. Bring the mixture to a boil and then reduce heat to simmer. Cook for an hour.

5. Add in the vegetables and cook for another hour.

6. Make a mixture of remaining broth and flour in a small mixing bowl.

7. Add this mixture, while stirring, into the Dutch oven to thicken the gravy.

8. When bubbly and thickened, take off heat.

18) Beef Stroganoff

A classic dish carrying all of the classic flavors
Cooking Time: **15 minutes**
Makes: 8 servings
List of Ingredients:
- 2 lb. of beef chuck roast, cut in strips
- Salt and pepper according to taste
- 1 tablespoon of oil
- 1 tablespoon of butter
- 2 cloves of garlic, minced
- ½ of medium onion, diced
- 8 oz. mushrooms, sliced
- 1 ½ tablespoons flour
- ½ cup white wine
- 2 cup of beef broth
- ¾ cup of crème fraiche
- 1 tablespoon chopped chives

Procedure:

1. Season the beef with salt and pepper.

2. Sear the meat on high heat in the Dutch oven for around 6 to 7 minutes. Take out the meat.

3. Add butter, onions and mushrooms in the same skillet and cook until the veggies are lightly browned.

4. Now put in garlic and let it fry for half a minute.

5. Add flour and keep stirring until well incorporated.

6. Pour in the wine and only a cup of stock. Make sure you scrape everything from the sides and the bottom of the pan.

7. Cook for 3 more minutes until sauce starts to thicken. Return the beef to the cooking pot and stir in remaining stock.

8. Bring it to simmering point, cover and cook for an hour.

9. In the end add in crème fraiche, chives and more salt and pepper if needed.

19) Pot Roast

A complete meal with rich flavors in one go
Cooking Time: **20 minutes**
Makes: 6 servings
List of Ingredients:
- 3 ½ lb. beef chuck roast
- 1 tablespoon oil
- Salt and pepper to taste
- 1 onion, chopped finely
- 1 clove of garlic, minced
- 2 ½ cups of beef stock
- 16 oz. canned tomatoes, diced
- ¼ cup of red wine vinegar
- 1 tablespoon of brown sugar
- 2 dried bay leaves
- 1 lb. small potatoes, quartered
- ¾ lb. carrots, diagonally sliced
- 6 oz. canned mushrooms
- 1 ½ tablespoons each of cold water and cornstarch
- 1 pinch each of thyme, dried basil and celery salt

Procedure:
1. Preheat your Dutch oven to 300 degrees.

2. Add oil in the oven and let it heat.

3. Season the meat and add it in the oven to cook for 5 or more minutes until browned from each side.

4. Take out meat and keep aside.

5. Now add onion and garlic to the oven and cook for 15 minutes.

6. When onions are translucent pour in the vinegar, stock, tomatoes, bay leaves and brown sugar.

7. Add meat and let it come to a boil. Cover and simmer for 4 – 4 ½ hours.

8. Add carrots and potatoes to the oven and cook for another 30 minutes.

9. Take out beef.

10. Add mushrooms and let the sauce thicken up after adding cornstarch and water slurry.

11. Lastly add celery salt, thyme and basil and serve this vegetable sauce with meat in a platter.

20) Vegetable Soup

This yields a creamy and enriched butternut and vegetable soup.

Cooking Time: 30 minutes

Makes: 6-8 servings

List of Ingredients:
- ¼ cup of vegetable oil
- 1 cup of onion, finely diced
- 2 teaspoons of garlic, minced
- 4 carrots, sliced thinly
- 2 cups of butternut squash, cubed
- 12 cups of vegetable broth
- 2 potatoes, cubed
- 2 ½ teaspoons thyme, dried
- Salt and pepper to taste
- 4 cups of kale leaves, finely chopped
- 16 oz. canned Northern beans, drained

Procedure:

1. Keep oven on medium heat. Add oil and let it heat up.

2. Add garlic and onion and cook till translucent.

3. Add in carrots and squash. Cook for around 15 minutes or until the squash starts to brown.

4. Add the broth and then add potatoes, seasonings and thyme. Let it come to boil and then let it simmer for around 45 minutes or until the vegetables are tender.

5. Mix in Kale and beans and cook for another 10 minutes.

6. Now pour 3 cups of this prepared soup into a blender and carefully blend the mixer using a kitchen towel on top of its pitcher.

7. After blending bring this mixture back to the Dutch oven to combine with the remaining chunky bit. This will bring the needed texture to the soup.

Chapter 2: Desserts

21) Strawberry Shortcake

This is an upside-down version of a kids' favorite delight.

Cooking Time: **20 minutes**

Makes: 8-10 servings

List of Ingredients:

- 1 cup of mini marshmallows
- 1 packet (3 oz.) strawberry flavored gelatin
- 1 package, (16 oz.) sliced frozen sweetened strawberries
- ½ cup of shortening
- 1 ½ cups of plain sugar
- 1 teaspoon of vanilla
- 3 medium eggs
- 2 ¼ cups of plain flour
- 1 cup of milk
- 3 teaspoons of baking powder

Procedure:

1. Preheat oven at 350 degrees.
2. Line the bottom of your Dutch oven with marshmallows.
3. Take a mixing bowl and mix together the frozen berries with the gelatin.

4. In another bowl, beat together the shortening and the sugar until creamy.

5. Add eggs, one by one, to the shortening mix and beat in between each addition.

6. Also add the vanilla and beat.

7. Sift together the dry ingredients and add it to the egg mixture, along with the milk.

8. Pour this prepared batter over the marshmallows in the oven and lastly spoon the strawberry mixture all over on top.

9. Bake for 40-50 minutes. Check with the toothpick to see if it comes out clean.

22) Shortcut To Apple Cobbler

Enjoy this short retake of apple cobbler

Cooking Time: **5 minutes**

Makes: 8-10 servings

List of Ingredients:

- 2 cans of cinnamon rolls with icing (refrigerated)
- 3 cans (21 oz. each) of apple pie filling

Procedure:

1. Preheat oven at 350 degrees.
2. Layer the bottom of the oven with pie filling.
3. Separate each cinnamon roll and then cut them in quarters before layering over the filling.
4. Bake only until golden brown from top.

23) Peanut Butter Bars

Sweet treats that carry the deathly combination of peanut butter and chocolate

Cooking Time: **15 minutes**

Makes: 12-15 servings

List of Ingredients:
- 1 cup each of butter, peanut butter, white sugar and brown sugar
- 2 large eggs
- ½ teaspoons of salt
- 1 teaspoon of baking soda
- 1 teaspoon of vanilla
- 2 cups each of plain flour and oats

For frosting
- ½ cup peanut butter
- 2 cups of chocolate chips

Procedure:

1. Preheat oven at 350 degrees.
2. Beat both the butters with both the sugars together with an electric beater.
3. Add eggs and incorporate.
4. Also add in vanilla and mix.

5. Sift and mix dry ingredients together before adding them to the butter mix.

6. Bake for 15-25 minutes or until slightly golden.

7. Melt the frosting ingredients together and mix well before spreading over the bars.

24) Peanut Butter And Apple Crisp

A nice twist to the apple crumble and a great dessert that can tag along in a family picnic basket anytime

Cooking Time: 15 minutes

Makes: 6-8 servings

List of Ingredients:
- 7 or 8 tart apples, (peeled, sliced)
- ¼ cup white sugar
- ½ cup of water
- 1 tablespoon of cinnamon
- 32 tablespoons of lemon juice
- ¾ cup each of plain flour and brown sugar
- ¼ cup margarine
- 1/3 cup of peanut butter

Procedure:

1. Preheat oven at 350 degrees.

2. Make a syrup of white sugar and water and then pour in lemon juice.

3. Arrange the slices of apple in the bottom of the Dutch oven.

4. Pour the sugar syrup on top and sprinkle cinnamon too.

5. In a mixing bowl mix together the remaining ingredients, until it gives a crumb texture.

6. Spread the 'crumb' all over the apples and bake for 40 minutes or until nicely crisp and golden.

25) Marshmallow Cookie Bars

This creamy and gooey dessert is going to remind you of sticky s'mores that you once enjoyed at campfires.

Cooking Time: **20 minutes**

Makes: 12-15 servings

List of Ingredients:

- 1 cup each of mini marshmallows, butterscotch chips and semi-sweet chocolate chips
- 3 cups of graham cracker crumbs
- ¾ cup of softened margarine
- 1 can (14 oz.) sweetened condensed milk

Procedure:

1. Preheat oven to 350 degrees.

2. Mix together the crumbs and the margarine and then press the mixture in the bottom of your Dutch oven.

3. Next, make an even layer of butterscotch chips, chocolate chips and marshmallows on top, followed by an even coating of condensed milk.

4. Bake for 25 minutes till it becomes bubbly on top.

Easy Ramen Noodle Snacks

Fast Chicken Noodle Soup

Ingredients:
- 8 oz. water
- 2 T oil
- 2 boneless chicken breasts, cooked, cubed
- 1 carrot, shredded
- 1 C shredded cabbage
- 2 T minced garlic
- 1 tsp. fresh ginger
- 4 packages ramen noodles
- **Soy sauce**

Directions:
1. Boil water and add cooked chicken, and vegetables, ramen noodles, and cook for about 3 minutes or so
2. Season to taste with soy sauce

Peanut Chicken Noodles

Ingredients:
- Ramen noodles
- ½ C chicken stock
- 3 T creamy peanut butter
- ½ tsp salt and pepper to taste
- 1 can light coconut milk
- 3 C cooked, shredded chicken breasts
- 2 C diced cabbage
- ¼ C cilantro leaves
- 1 serrano chile, sliced
- **2 T srirarcha**

Directions:
1. Cook the ramen noodles, drain and set aside (saving boiling water
2. Heat the stock and 4 more ingredients and boil in medium saucepan
3. *Add the cooking water, chicken and milk and cook for about 3 minutes, or until hot, add cabbage and noodles, wait for cabbage to wilt.*
4. Cook for few minutes and serve

Rice And Shrimp

Ingredients:
- 2 packages ramen noodles
- 2 tsp sesame oil
- 2 tsp canola oil
- 4 oz. shitake mushrooms
- 4 C vegetable broth
- 2 C carrots, shredded
- 1 C ginger, 4ths
- ½ lbs shrimp, peeled, deveined
- 2 C sliced scallions
- 2 tsp lime juice
- 1 ½ tsp soy sauce
- 2 T fresh cilantro
- 2 T mint leaves
- **¼ C unsalted peanuts, halved**

Directions:
1. Boil water, add noodles and boil, then set aside
2. Toss the noodles and sesame oil in a skillet
3. *Add oil to pan and sauté mushrooms, carrots, ginger, broth and other vegetables, herbs and soy sauce*
4. Add soup over noodles and serve

Spinach And Ramen Noodles

Ingredients:
- 2 packages beef ramen noodles, with seasoning
- 1 C baby spinach
- 2 scallions, sliced
- **1 carrot, shredded**

Directions:
1. Cook the ramen noodles per the instruction, with beef seasoning
2. Add in spinach until wilted, scallions and carrots
3. *Season to taste and enjoy*

Vegan Ramen Salad

Ingredients:
- 1 package ramen noodles
- 1 C romaine lettuce shredded
- 1 can water chestnuts, drained
- **Salt and pepper to taste**

Directions:
1. Prepare ramen noodles per package with seasoning
2. Slice chestnuts and lettuce
3. *Toss everything together with salt and pepper and enjoy*

Veggie Ramen Ii

Ingredients:
- 1 T butter
- 2 T sliced carrots
- 2 T green beans
- 2 T white corn
- 2 T edamame
- Pork ramen noodles
- **2 C water**

Directions:
1. Cook your 2 T vegetables and add ramen noodles with the water until ramen noodles are cooked
2. Add seasoning and stir
3. Serve

Foo Ramen

Ingredients:
- 1 egg
- 1 T water
- 2 C boiling water
- 1 package ramen noodles
- **Green onions, sliced garnish**

Directions:
1. Whisk an egg with 1 T water together and set aside.
2. Bring boiling water in saucepan and add egg, then the noodles, cook until tender
3. *Season with packet seasoning, garnish with onions*
    4. Serve

Chicken Salad

Ingredients
- ¼ head cabbage
- 1 chicken breast, cooked and diced
- ¼ white onion, diced
- 1 package ramen noodles, crushed
- 2 T oil
- 2 T white vinegar
- **2 T sugar**

Directions:
1. Shred the chicken and cabbage, add in crushed ramen, whisk in seasoning with other ingredients, boil, toss and serve.

Mandarin Ramen Salad

Ingredients:
- 1 package ramen noodles, chicken flavor
- 1 package coleslaw mixture
- 2 sliced celery sliced
- 1 can mandarin oranges
- 2 T white vinegar
- **2 T sugar**

Directions:
1. Cook your ramen noodles just as directed on package.
2. Stir pol with ramen seasoning,
3. *Toss cooked ramen with the slaw mixture and vinegar seasoning and sugar*
4. Garish to taste and serve.

Thai Ramen

Ingredients:
- 1 packet pork flavored ramen noodles
- ½ tsp peanut butter
- 1 lime, juiced
- ½ tsp soy sauce
- **Garlic onion powder to taste**

Directions:
1. Cook ramen noodles, according to package, drain most of water
2. Add seasoning and remaining ingredients and stir well.
3. Garnish to taste and serve

Ramen Lasagna

Ingredients:
- 4 packages uncooked ramen noodles, no seasoning
- Cooked Italian sausage
- 1 jar spaghetti sauce, your preference
- Chopped spinach
- **Mozzarella cheese**

Directions:
1. Spray baking dish, and add 4 squares uncooked ramen noodles
2. Top with ground, cooked Italian sausage
3. *Add chopped spinach*
4. Top with spaghetti sauce
5. **Top with cheese**
6. Cover pan with foil and bake for 35-40 minutes at 350 degrees
7. Take out 10-15 minutes before serving

Shrimp And Chili

Ingredients:
- 1 package chili ramen noodles
- ¼ C diced scallions
- 1 C cooked shrimp
- **Lime wedge**

Directions:
1. Cook the ramen according to package
2. Toss with scallions, shrimp and wedge
3. *Serve*

Ham Fried Ramen Noodles

Ingredients:
- Pork ramen noodles
- 1 T sesame oil
- 1 T olive oil
- ¼ C diced ham
- **¼ C frozen peas and carrots**

Directions:
1. Cook noodles, and drain.
2. In separate skillet heat oils and remaining ingredients
3. *When cooked at to noodles and toss*
4. Garnish to taste and serve

Parmesan Noodles

Ingredients:
- 1 package ramen noodles
- 1 T butter
- **¼ C grated parmesan cheese**

Directions:
1. Make ramen noodles per packet directions, no seasoning
2. Drain and add butter
3. *Top with parmesan and serve*

Homemade Chicken And Noodles

Ingredients:
- 1-2 packages ramen noodles
- 1 C chicken broth
- 1 C shredded chicken breast
- **Crinkle cut carrots slices**

Directions
1. Cook ramen noodles per instructions
2. Add noodles to chicken broth and add remaining ingredients
3. Let simmer and enjoy

Semarang Kopyok Noodles

Ingredients
- 400 grams of lomi brewed
- 150 grams of bean sprouts are brewed
- 4 lontong pieces cut into pieces
- 4 garlic cloves are smoothed
- 200 ml of water

Gravy ingredients
- 1 liter of chicken broth
- 1 teaspoon of powdered chicken broth
- 1 teaspoon of salt
- Sufficient pepper powder

Supplementary material

- 8 small fried tofu pieces
- 1 fine celery stick sliced
- 1 tablespoon of fried shallots
- 4 pieces of crackers gendar crushed roughly
- 2 tablespoons of sweet soy sauce

How to make

1. Boil the broth until boiling. Add pepper, chicken powder broth, and salt. Stir until evenly distributed then set aside.
2. Put the rice cake, lomi, bean sprouts, and tofu into a dish, then pour the sauce into it, sprinkle with celery slices, fried onions, serve with sweet soy sauce and crackers gendar.
3. Serve it.

Riau Lendir Noodles

Ingredients

- 500 grams of wet yellow noodles
- 100 grams of peanuts
- 1 tablespoon of fine ginger
- 1 medium size java sugar block
- 200 grams of bean sprouts
- enough chili is thinly sliced
- enough celery leaves thinly sliced
- 2 tablespoons cornstarch
- 500 ml of water
- 4 boiled chicken eggs

Softened seasoning

- 4 cloves garlic

- 3 red onion cloves
- 10 red chilies

How to make

1. Fried peanuts, then coarse blender.
2. Heat the oil, sauté with a small amount of seasoned cooking oil. Add the blended beans, then pour the water, mix well, then slice the sliced java sugar, stir again until evenly mixed.
3. Pour cornstarch that has been given water, give salt and flavoring, then stir until evenly mixed.
4. Soak bean sprouts with hot water until half cooked.
5. Serve noodles, bean sprouts, boiled eggs in a dish / bowl, sprinkle celery leaves, and give cayenne pepper, then flush with gravy.
6. Mucus noodles are ready to serve.

Makasar Titi Noodles

Ingredients
- 400 grams of egg noodles
- 200 grams of chicken meat, cut into small pieces
- 150 grams of peeled shrimp
- 100 grams of beef liver, cut into pieces
- 5 meatballs, cut into 4 parts
- 2 sticks of carrot, thinly sliced lengthwise
- 100 grams of green mustard, cut into pieces
- 50 grams of cabbage, sliced roughly
- 1 onion, sliced
- 1 egg
- 1 tomato
- 2 sticks of celery leaves
- 2 stems of leeks
- Cooking oil
- Sufficient cornmeal flour

Softened seasoning

- 8 garlic cloves, finely chopped
- ½ teaspoon of pepper powder
- 1 teaspoon of paprika powder
- 1 teaspoon of salt

Supplementary Ingredients

- Lime
- Fried onion to taste
- Bottled chili sauce

How to make

1. Boil the noodles until they cook, remove and drain
2. Heat cooking oil, then fry the noodles on medium heat until browned and crispy.
3. Boil the chicken meat until done take the broth, then lift and diced chicken meat.
4. Heat stir-fried cooking oil mashed until fragrant. Add the shrimp and chicken pieces, stir until cooked, then pour the broth into it.
5. Enter also beef liver, meatballs, cabbage, mustard greens, and carrots. Mix well until the vegetables are slightly wilted.
6. Add the cornstarch solution, stir until it bursts and the water thickens slightly.
7. Put the eggs in it, mix well. Lift.

8. Place the noodles on the plate, then pour the sauce and the contents.
9. Serve while hot.

Malang Cwie Noodles

Ingredients
- **500 grams of noodles for chicken noodles**
- **1 bunch of lettuce**

Additional ingredients

- **200 grams of finely chopped chicken meat**
- **5 garlic cloves, finely chopped**
- **1 teaspoon of sesame oil**
- **1 teaspoon of pepper powder**
- **1 tablespoon of sweet soy sauce**
- **Salt to taste**
- **Right amount of oil**

Gravy ingredients

- **4 cloves of garlic, finely chopped**
- **3 cm of ginger, crushed**
- **1 liter of chicken broth**
- **1 teaspoon of pepper powder**
- **1 teaspoon of sesame oil**
- **Beef meatballs according to taste**
- **Salt to taste**
- **Right amount of oil**

Supplementary material

- **Fried dumpling skin**
- **Fried onions**
- **Chili sauce**

How to make

1. Boil the noodles, remove and drain.
2. Heat cooking oil and sesame oil, sauté garlic until fragrant. Add minced chicken, pepper, salt and sweet soy sauce. Stir until the spices soak, lift and set aside.
3. Make the sauce, sauté the garlic and ginger until fragrant. Add the broth water, add salt, pepper, and sesame oil, cook until boiling.
4. Add meatballs, cook meatballs until floating. Lift and set aside.
5. Serve noodles and lettuce in a bowl, give stir-fried chicken, stir fried, then flush with meatball sauce.
6. Serve noodles with fried dumplings and chili sauce

Kwetiau Fried Noodles

Ingredients
- ½ kg of rice noodles
- 2 eggs
- Caisim to taste
- 3 thinly sliced meatballs
- 100 grams of shredded chicken meat

Softened seasoning

- 2 garlic cloves, chopped
- ½ teaspoon of powdered broth
- ½ teaspoon pepper powder
- Sweet soy sauce to taste
- Salt to taste

How to make

1. Saute the garlic until fragrant, add the eggs and make scrambled.
2. Add the vegetables, meatballs, shredded chicken, mix well, add salt, pepper powder, and powder broth, stir again.
3. Add the noodles stir well, then pour the sweet soy sauce to taste, stir again until smooth and the spices soak.
4. Lift and serve

Javanese Kwetiau Fried Noodles

Ingredients
- 500 grams of dry / wet rice noodles
- 1 egg
- 2 celery sticks, long slices
- 1 lap chiong stem, round slices
- 50 grams of cabbage, sliced roughly
- 2 tablespoons sweet soy sauce
- Salt to taste
- Adequate sugar
- Pepper to taste

Softened seasoning

- 3 garlic cloves
- 5 red onion cloves
- 10 cayenne fruit
- 2 pecan nuts
- 1 tablespoon of ebi rinsed with water

How to make

1. Boil the rice noodles, remove and drain. Then give 1 tablespoon of sweet soy sauce and 1 tablespoon of cooking oil. Stir until evenly mixed.
2. Sauté the spices until fragrant, add the chiong and egg, then stir it scrambled.
3. Add cabbage and celery, add salt, sugar, pepper, mix well.
4. Add the noodles, add a little water, stir evenly and the spices soak.
5. Lift and serve with a sprinkling of fried onions and pickles.

Fried Seafood Kwetiau Noodles

Ingredients
- 200 grams of rice
- 2 caisim sticks, cut into pieces
- 100 grams of bean sprouts
- 3 garlic cloves, then chopped fried
- 2 tablespoons of soy sauce
- 1 tablespoon sweet soy sauce
- 1 tablespoon fish sauce
- 1/2 teaspoon of pepper
- 1 stem of leeks, sliced
- Right amount of oil
- 5 meatballs, slices
- 100 grams of peeled shrimp
- 100 grams of fishcake, sliced

How to make

1. Heat cooking oil, add meatballs, shrimp, fishcake, stir until the shrimp changes color.
2. Add the rice noodles, soy sauce, sweet soy sauce, fish and pepper sauce. Then pour a little water. Mix well until the color of the noodles is brown.
3. Add the bean sprouts and fried onions along with the broiled oil. Stir until cooked.
4. Lift and serve.

Chicken Fried Kwetiau Noodles

Ingredients

- 500 grams of wet rice noodles
- Fish meatballs according to taste
- Raw chicken according to taste
- 1 egg
- 50 grams of cabbage, sliced roughly
- 2 stems of leeks
- 1 tablespoon of margarine
- 1 tablespoon oyster sauce
- Water

Softened seasoning

- 2 Spring onions
- 3 garlic cloves
- 2 candlenuts

- 2 cayenne fruit
- Coriander to taste
- 1 tsp Pepper
- Flavoring

How to make

1. Boil the rice noodles, remove and drain.
2. Heat oil, sauté fine spices until fragrant. Add eggs for scrambled, then add chicken and meatballs, stir until blended.
3. Give a little water, sweet soy sauce, oyster sauce and flavoring. Add the noodles, cabbage and spring onions, then stir until cooked and evenly mixed.
4. Lift and serve.

Shrimp Fried Rice Noodles

Ingredients
- 300 grams of dried vermicelli
- 200 grams of peeled shrimp
- 2 eggs
- 4 tablespoon of sweet soy sauce
- 1 tablespoon of soy sauce
- Right amount of oil
- 100 ml of water
- 1 tie caisim, cut it into pieces

Softened seasoning

- 5 garlic cloves
- 2 Spring onions
- 1 teaspoon of pepper
- 1 tablespoon of dried ebi brew with water
- 1 teaspoon of salt
- ½ teaspoon of sugar

How to make

1. Bring rice noodles with warm water until soft, drain. Give sweet soy sauce, then stir until evenly mixed. Set it aside.

2. Heat cooking oil, sauté the seasoned spices until fragrant.
3. Add the shrimp and eggs then scrambled, until the shrimp changes color. Enter caisim and water. Let it boil.
4. Enter the vermicelli, stir well until cooked and the seasoning permeates.
5. Lift and serve.

www.ingramcontent.com/pod-product-compliance
Lightning Source LLC
Chambersburg PA
CBHW071441070526
44578CB00001B/173